PROVENCE

Text by Michèle Aué

Translated by Alison Hebborn

CONTENTS

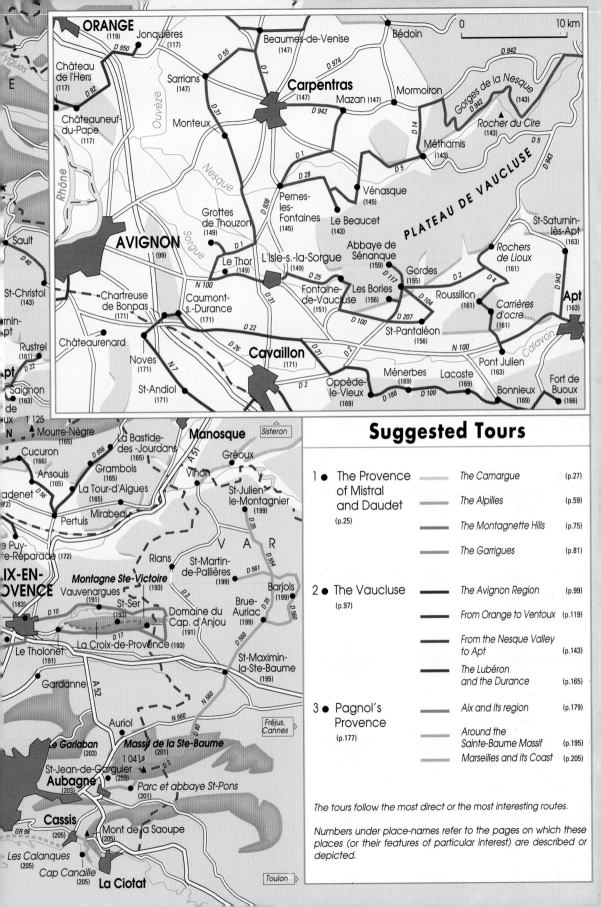

ORANGE (119)
Jonquières (117)
Château de l'Hers (117)
Sarrians (147)
Châteauneuf-du-Pape (117)
Monteux
Beaumes-de-Venise (147)
Bédoin
CARPENTRAS (147)
Mazan (147)
Mormoiron
Gorges de la Nesque
Rocher du Cire (143)
Méthamis (143)
Pernes-les-Fontaines (145)
Vénasque (145)
PLATEAU DE VAUCLUSE
St-Saturnin-lès-Apt (163)
Grottes de Thouzon (149)
Le Beaucet (143)
Rochers de Lioux (161)
AVIGNON (99)
Abbaye de Sénanque (159)
Gordes (155)
Roussillon (161)
Carrières d'ocre (161)
Apt (163)
Le Thor (149)
L'Isle-s.-la-Sorgue (149)
Fontaine-de-Vaucluse (151)
Les Bories (156)
Sault
Chartreuse de Bonpas (171)
St-Christol (143)
Caumont-s.-Durance (171)
St-Pantaléon (156)
Châteaurenard
Noves (171)
CAVAILLON (171)
Rustrel (161)
St-Andiol (171)
Pont Julien (163)
Fort de Buoux (166)
Saignon (163)
Oppède-le-Vieux (169)
Ménerbes (169)
Lacoste (169)
Bonnieux (169)

Mourre-Nègre (165)
Manosque
Sisteron
Cucuron (166)
La Bastide-des-Jourdans (165)
Gréoux
Ansouis (165)
Grambois (165)
Vinon
La Tour-d'Aigues (165)
St-Julien-le-Montagnier (199)
Pertuis
Mirabeau
V A R
Le Puy-e-Réparade (172)
Rians
St-Martin-de-Pallières (199)
Barjols (199)
AIX-EN-PROVENCE (183)
Montagne Ste-Victoire (193)
Vauvenargues (191)
St-Ser (193)
Domaine du Cap. d'Anjou (191)
Brue-Auriac (199)
La Croix-de-Provence (193)
Le Tholonet (191)
St-Maximin-la-Ste-Baume (195)
Gardanne
Auriol
Fréjus, Cannes
Le Garlaban (203)
Massif de la Ste-Baume (201)
St-Jean-de-Garguier (203)
Aubagne (203)
Parc et abbaye St-Pons (201)
Cassis (205)
Mont de la Saoupe (205)
Les Calanques (205)
Cap Canaille (205)
La Ciotat
Toulon

Suggested Tours

1 ● The Provence of Mistral and Daudet (p.25)

2 ● The Vaucluse (p.97)

3 ● Pagnol's Provence (p.177)

The Camargue (p.27)
The Alpilles (p.59)
The Montagnette Hills (p.75)
The Garrigues (p.81)
The Avignon Region (p.99)
From Orange to Ventoux (p.119)
From the Nesque Valley to Apt (p.143)
The Lubéron and the Durance (p.165)
Aix and its region (p.179)
Around the Sainte-Baume Massif (p.195)
Marseilles and its Coast (p.205)

The tours follow the most direct or the most interesting routes.

Numbers under place-names refer to the pages on which these places (or their features of particular interest) are described or depicted.

1

TWO THOUSAND YEARS OF SUN

RHONE AND MISTRAL

FROM PROVINCIA TO PROVENCE

1

RHONE AND MISTRAL

How could anyone criticise Van Gogh for the intensity of his colours, the vibrant fullness of his sketches or the scorching luminosity of his skies? For his portraits of Provence – of shaggy irises, grey-green olive trees and midnight blue suns – exaggerate nothing. Provence opens expansively onto the Mediterranean, breathing in salty sea air through the yawning delta of its river, *Lou Rose* (the Rhone), while its coastline is cut into jagged ribbons by long indigo blue inlets to the east, and caressed by silky soft waves lapping at its offshore bars to the west, where Le Grau-du-Roi and Port-Camargue lie coiled together.

The Camargue and Crau Plains were both built by rivers. For one, the Rhone laid down soft silty alluvium in the waters of Vaccarès Lagoon between its *Grand* and *Petit* arms, while, for the other, the Durance, which was once a great river surging towards the Mediterranean through Lamanon Ravine, banked up gravel and pebbles into an alluvial cone.

Beyond the plains, set in parallel waves pressed in by the great unyielding arc of the Alps, the mountain ranges of Provence lift the lacy white expanses of their cliff faces towards the sky. From the mountains of Marseilleveyre and Estaque, Sainte-Baume and Sainte-Victoire, Montagnette, the Alpilles and the Lubéron, to the Vaucluse Plateau and Mont Ventoux, the ranges rise as a series of so many obstacles, the silhouette of their mineral spines scoring bold white lines across the sky. The deep, fertile soils of the low valleys that spread out in soft contours between the chains are home to oak and pine forests, silver-leafed olive groves,

A lavender field near Sault

neat rows of violet-blue cushions of lavender bushes, and fragrant orchards of sweet almonds and golden apricots.

Provence is a land of limestone, that permeable, and surprisingly fragile, rock. Its mountains are riddled with swallow holes, cut into gorges and hewn into canyons by rivers such as the Nesque and the Régalon. Sometimes, the mountain captures its runoff rainwaters and, abandoning its surface to the burning sun, hides them in the mysterious intricacies of its depths, only to release them again suddenly, at the foot of its cliffs, as gushing springs. The spring at Vaucluse is so typical an example of this kind of resurgent underground river that it has become the universal reference for this geological feature. Although its landscapes are coloured predominantly in brilliant whites, Provence boasts some remarkable exceptions, such as the scarlet and saffron-yellow ravines that run through the ochre-red lands of Roussillon, where so vivid a palette of natural colours once more calls Van Gogh to mind.

Due to its southerly latitude, Provence enjoys the kind of climate that is generally thought of as virtually ideal. Of course, as with any natural phenomenon, this idealistic view must be tempered, just a little, in order to avoid any excessive claims. Nevertheless, with an exceptional 2,500 hours of sunshine per year, the essential characteristic of these open Mediterranean lands remains their sun-drenched quality. As if the region had been blessed by the gods, the long summer days, under the very stable influence of a Saharan-centred anticyclone, stretch into months of hot, dry weather. But, while sun-worshipping tourists can satisfy their instinctive desires for basking lazily on the beaches, Provence's horticulturists and market gardeners are forced to seek out the deepest water tables, dig wells and channels, harness springs and store up supplies, as, in any land cursed by drought, they are reminded once again of the true value of those pearls of great price that pour from the tap – so readily taken for granted in a less parched land.

Rustrel: The Provençal Colorado

And yet, Provence also has its fair share of rainfall. In fact, with an average of six hundred millimetres per year, it gets as much as Paris. The only, albeit considerable, difference is that here the rain is spread unevenly throughout the year, with autumn as the wet season. Damp air laden with fine drizzle, so common in northern climes, is unknown here. Provence's autumn storms are wild and violent, unleashing huge quantities of water in veritable downpours. No longer meeting with resistance from the summer anticyclone which has moved southwards again, moisture-laden depressions blown in on westerly winds pour down, relentlessly, onto the Rhone valley and Provence's mountains, provoking lethal mood swings in the region's waterways. The Ouvèze, the Aigues and the Durance change suddenly from peaceful rivers whose turquoise waters tumble boisterously over their rocky beds, to roaring muddy monsters, bent on destruction, their raging torrents swallowing up banks, dykes, bridges, roads and houses alike.

Next come the clear, bright skies of the cold season, when the mistral – the *grand balayeur*, or great sweeper, whose name, from the word *maître*, means master – comes into its own. Cypress trees bow down and the whole of Provence shivers as the mistral blows in from the north. Violent and unpredictable, it lashes out suddenly only to stop again just as abruptly. Then at last, the mistral's icy blasts and the storms blown in from the Atlantic give way to spring, as the first gentle days of hesitant sunshine bring an early sweetness to the air.

From the earliest days of human history, the people of Provence have instilled their beloved homeland with its own unique traditions, colourful folklore and distinctive character. Today, its many delights include the flower market at Aix-en-Provence, *santon* figurines, salt from the Camargue, the regular pattern of its rice fields, the legendary Tarasque monster, the bridge at Avignon, the beauty of its coastal inlets, azure skies, rasping cicadas, and the venerable Daudet's *Letters From My Mill*.

The Two Sovereign Lords of Provence

The **mistral** is a cold north-northwest wind that blows the length of the Rhone corridor before it opens out, howling, onto the plains of the delta, and is lost in the bright Mediterranean distance. This violent wind can blow up to two hundred and fifty kilometres per hour. It is hardly surprising then, that here, in a land subject to the constant vagaries of a particularly blustery wind rose, it bears the name *mistrau*, or *mistral*, meaning master wind. At the top of Mont Ventoux, that desolate land of stone and wind, an archeological site has yielded up curved fragments of pottery – the remains of little spiral trumpets. The theory that this was once a votive altar where these trumpets were blown to appease the anger of the master wind seems to be borne out by the discovery, near Saint-Jean-de-Garguier, of another collection of these little *toutouros*, which are used, on Saint John's day, in processions that bear the most outrageous marks of paganism. The great torrent of the **Rhone**, calmed only slightly by its passage through the Alpine lakes, surges southwards and, foaming and majestic, opens out onto the plains of the Comtat (county of) Venaissin. At the foot of the twin fortresses of Beaucaire and Tarascon, its tremendous flow has been known, in periods of high water, to exceed two thousand cubic metres a second, due in part to the Aigues, the Ouvèze, the Sorgue, the Durance and the Gard which all reinforce its torrent with their own violent and sudden floodwaters. Finally, becoming sluggish under the weight of the silt it carries, it divides and wanders off into the plain where, losing its remaining strength, the triangle of its delta opens onto the fabulous landscape of the Camargue.

1 Bouillabaisse

2 Olives in a Provençal market

3 Soupe au pistou

4 Calissons from Aix-en-Provence

5 Berlingots from Carpentras

"À La Provençale..."

All the fragrances and colours of the sunburnt, windswept land of Provence are concentrated in its cuisine. No place here for blandness or boredom! Instead, a hint of garlic and the rich aroma of smooth, golden-green olive oil join together to bring out the full flavours of fish and vegetables in explosions of subtle taste. The place of honour at the Provençal table is reserved for the *aïoli*, a garlic mayonnaise, where eggs, oil, and juicy crushed garlic swell into folds of creamy softness. *Aïoli* also gives its name to the dish of cod and snails to which it is the indispensable accompaniment. When talking of Provençal cuisine, it is essential to avoid that unpardonable error of confusing *soupe de poissons, bourride and bouillabaisse.* Ground and milled, *soupe de poissons* becomes a thick fish soup laced with garlicky croutons. For a good *bourride*, white fish – bass, angler fish and whiting – are cooked in court-bouillon, and arranged on slices of garlicky toast, before a light and foamy *aïoli*, thinned with the court-bouillon, then reduced, is poured over them. But for the greatest of these culinary delights, the incomparable and beloved *bouillabaisse*, rockfish – scorpion fish, conger eels and monk fish – and seafood – *langoustines* (large prawns) and mussels from Bouzigues – are the essential ingredients. Its secret lies in its name. Requiring an expert eye and a skillful turn of hand, not often readily shared, the divine blend of oil and stock is created by repeatedly and alternately bringing it to the boil (*bouillir*) and lowering (*baisser*) the heat. In the Nîmes region, cod is scalded, flaked, and moistened with olive oil and milk, to become a *brandade* – meaning, in the old Provençal dialect, a well-mixed paste – where the strong fish flavour blends with the perfumes of olives and truffles and the richness of creamy milk. Salad vegetables are served with *anchoïade* (a kind of anchovy paste), *tapenade* (a blend of black olives, capers, anchovies and olive oil), and *rouille* (a chili-hot aïoli), and sprinkled with fine sprigs of dried thyme, savory, rosemary and marjoram – the bouquet of herbs together known as the *Herbes de Provence*. If *soupe au pistou* gets its delicious flavour from basil, its name gives no hint of it. The *pistou* is, in fact, the pestle used to crush the basil, garlic and olive oil in the mortar. A little pasta swelling in the broth makes this rich dish a meal in itself. Much simpler, but just as tasty, is *aïgo boulido*, a bread and egg dish which was, traditionally, poor man's fare. In order for *boeuf en daube* to deserve its name, the choicest pieces of beef must be simmered gently in red wine in a tightly sealed pot. The gardens of Provence yield a bright profusion of fresh vegetables – courgettes, sweet peppers, artichokes, fennel, aubergines, onions and tomatoes – which in turn give mouthwatering ratatouilles, stuffed vegetables, fritters, and *tians* – tasty gratins mixed with a handful of rice. And no Provençal meal is complete without the sweet taste of Mediterranean fruit. The thirteen guests at the Last Supper – Jesus and the twelve apostles – are remembered in the thirteen desserts traditionally served on Christmas Eve: grapes, figs, almonds, walnuts, pears, apples, crystalised apricots, quince jelly, winter melons, and, of course, succulent *pompe à huile, calissons* from Aix-en-Provence (lozenge-shaped marzipan delights covered in white icing), and black nougat and white nougat from Montélimar. Then there are crunchy *oreillettes* and *chichis*, sprinkled with sugar, and little oval-shaped *navettes*, browned to perfection, not to forget the pretty multicoloured *berlingots*, or boiled sweets, from Carpentras. And, finally, to wash it all down, a little local wine, probably a rosé, can be chosen from among the many produced in the region: a Gigondas or a Châteauneuf-du-Pape, a Rasteau or a Beaumes-de-Venise, a Tavel, a Listel or perhaps a delicately fruity Bandol.

2

FROM PROVINCIA TO PROVENCE

Bearing witness to its Neolithic past, Provence still boasts the remains of the surprisingly sophisticated wooden cabins that were built as its population adopted a sedentary way of life, opened clearings in the oak and pine forests, and began cultivating and defending this, their chosen land. One of the earliest settlements of this kind was discovered near Courthézon, to the north of Avignon, in the rich alluvial plain between the Rhone and the Ouvèze.

Next came those little-known tribes, the Ligurians and the Celts, who established their fortified settlements on the heights of natural escarpments. Today, the remains of their civilisations can be admired in the *oppida* at Saint-Blaise, Allauch, Baou Rous and, in particular, Entremont. Fearsome warriors, they would attach the irrefutable proof of their courage – human skulls taken in battle – to the necks of their mounts, or arrange them in decorative groups around their portals and in their houses. But, for all their formidable strength, even they were unable to resist the gradual invasion, from about 600 B.C., of those seafaring people from Phocaea, on the coast of Asia Minor, who came determined to establish a trading post here, on the sheltered shores of Lacydon Bay. Under these enterprising Greeks, Massalia soon became a veritable Phocaean colony, steeped in Hellenic culture and tradition.

The Massalians, worried by the presence of the native Celts, who were little inclined to respect any lasting peace, and concerned with the defence of this coastline of flourishing orchards, olive groves and vineyards, made the shrewd decision of forming an alliance with a certain up-and-coming young city – Rome. The Romans, secretly nurturing plans to establish their rule over these pleasant Mediterranean shores, seized upon this invitation to Provence as the opportunity they had been waiting for, and, in about 125 B.C., their disciplined and efficient troops freed Greek Massalia from the ever increasing threat posed by the Salian tribes, destroying their capital city, Entremont, and scattering its population.

In order to govern this region, whose position between Italy and Spain made it one of major strategic importance, *Aquæ Sextiæ*, the future Aix-en-Provence, and, further to the west, the nerve centre of this *provincia romana*, Narbonne, were founded. Although allied with Rome, Massalia remained independent, a small Hellenic outpost in the heart of vast Roman territories. Massalia played its diplomatic cards carefully in its dealings with its ambitious ally, but politics is a dangerous game and, having sided with Pompey against Caesar, it was forced, when Caesar triumphed, to bear the bitter consequences of its treasonous acts. In 49 B.C., Massalia fell to Rome, and, demoted to the rank of a simple *colonia latina*, was struck into mute submission.

But at the same time, the golden age of the *Pax Romana*, the Roman Peace, dawned in *Provincia* (Provence), bringing with it a period of fabulous prosperity under that most august of emperors, who, naming himself Augustus, decreed that he was to be worshipped as a god. But then, Romanisation seemed a small price to pay for the opportunities and advantages offered by the Romans, for whom material comfort and a refined aesthetic sense (as demonstrated in their temples, like the one at Château-Bas) went hand in hand. Many fine cities prospered under the Romans: *Aquæ Sextiæ*, Aix-en-Provence; *Arelate*, Arles; *Nemausus*, Nîmes; the very fine *Glanum*; *Avennio*, the future Avignon; *Cabellio*, Cavaillon; *Arausio*, Orange; *Carpentoracte*, Carpentras; *Apta*, Apt; *Vasio*, Vaison-la-Romaine; and many more besides. As these towns grew, they not only acquired all the latest modern conveniences – drains, fountains, aqueducts (such as the astonishing Pont du Gard), baths, hypocausts and *domus* – they also collected many grandiose monuments built to Rome's glory – triumphal arches, theatres, amphitheatres, porticos, temples and mausoleums.

Five centuries of peace brought the Romanisation of *Provincia* to its height, while records clearly show that the rapid progress made by Christianity had, by the end of the 3rd century, already established a number of dioceses in the region. As the barbarians swept through the whole of western Europe, Provence was, at first, spared to some extent, as the conquering armies, passing by disinterestedly, seemed to ignore it. But when the last Roman emperor, the young Romulus Augustulus, was deposed in 476 A.D., the Visigoths and the Burgundians divided Provence between them. First harried, then routed, they, in turn, finally surrendered to the Franks, under Clovis, and Provence, so coveted a land, and so easy a prey, was torn apart by the fratricidal struggles between Clovis' successors. Only in the 11th century, when Provence became part of the Holy Roman Empire, did the region, subject for years to Saracen incursions, find peace and tranquillity once more.

To the west of the Rhone, the Counts of Toulouse had made Saint-Gilles the cradle of their dynasty but, after their tangles with the French monarchy during the Albigensian Crusade in the early 13th century, all their lands, from the right bank of the Rhone as far as Beaucaire, fell under royal rule. And, since the king, Saint Louis, had made the clever move of marrying his brother, Charles I of Anjou, to Beatrice, heiress to the Count of Provence, the monarchy began to take a closer interest in the rest of the region. It was hardly surprising then, that the saintly king should choose to set out, on both his Holy Crusades, from his brand new port at Aigues-Mortes. And so it was that, in the 13th century, the golden age of the Angevin dynasty dawned in Provence.

Glanum: The Antiques - The mausoleum

Beaucaire: The castle

Although it was to leave an indelible mark on Provence, the establishment of the papacy at Avignon, was, in fact, due more to fortuitous circumstances than to any carefully laid plan. In 1274, in return for their good and faithful service during the war with the southern Lords, accused of heresy, the French monarchy gave the Comtat Venaissin and its capital, Venasque, to the popes. With Rome in the grip of bitterly disputed internal quarrels, the popes chose to settle nearby, in the noble town of Avignon, under the protection of the Counts of Provence. From 1314 onwards, Clement V retired regularly to his monastery at Groseau, where the surging waters pounded at the cliffs, while his successor, John XXII, former Bishop of Avignon, chose to end his days behind the solid crenellated walls of his old see. Stern and realistic, Benedict XII, with no thought of returning to Saint Peter's holy city, built an elegant but impregnable fortress and called it, with just a hint of arrogance, the Papal Palace. In 1348, as a terrible outbreak of plague dev-astated the country, Clement VI, taking advantage of the troubles that assailed Queen Joan I of Anjou, bought Avignon from her. Then came Innocent VI and Urban V, who, with Gregory XI, began to think more and more about returning to Rome. Through the dark days of a chaotic period which was to last for nearly thirty years, pope fought antipope for the right to represent God on earth with successive and reciprocal pronouncements of excommunication. Only in 1403 did the papacy return to the Holy City, never again to leave.

Both the County of Provence and the Comtat Venaissin had prospered on this pontifical manna and, despite the plague that had raged in endemic fashion since 1348, despite famine and roaming bands of plundering mercenaries, and despite the bloody rebellion of the Lords of the Alpilles and the Lubéron, life somehow went on. By the end of the reign of Good King René, Provence began, at last, to experience a period of peaceful prosperity and domesticity, far removed from the youthfully grand politi-

Avignon: The Papal Palace - The ceiling in the Stag Room

cal ambitions of its now much wiser sovereign. Succeeding René to the throne, his nephew offered Provence to his cousin, King Louis XI, and, in 1481, the County of Provence became, once and for all, the property of the French crown. Its capital, Aix-en-Provence, acquired a Parliament, and Marseilles became the great Mediterranean port it is today. All manner of exports from the East passed through it, and with them, the bubonic plague. In 1720, an epidemic devastated the entire region and nothing, not even the gigantic plague wall, built between Lagnes and Méthamis, was able to halt its advance.

Later, it was to the robust accents of *The War Song of the Rhine Army*, by Rouget de Lisle, that, in response to the stirring "fatherland in danger" declaration of 1792, an army of five hundred volunteers from Marseilles trooped into Paris, giving their name to the French national anthem – *La Marseillaise*. But it was Mistral who, with *Mirèio*, revived Provence's tongue, so full of sun and the song of cicadas.

Maillane: Frédéric Mistral's tomb

Parlez-Vous Oc?

As any true native of Marseilles knows, a Parisian *parla pounchu* – speaks with a clipped accent. When, in an attempt to make themselves understood and obeyed throughout the kingdom, the royal authorities imposed the French language on the nation, the people of Provence, faithful to their old Oc language and not about to let it die, developed their own distinctive tongue, whose singing accent and colourful turns of phrase barely disguised its Occitan roots. You must *bouléguer* a salad to dress it in its fragrant golden coat of olive oil, and be careful not to get *ensuqué* by the hot southern sun. In 1854, at Font-Ségugne Castle, seven young poets, including a certain Frédéric Mistral, came to the defence of the Oc language – by then reduced to the ranks of a simple dialect, an oral tradition, or even sometimes derogatorily referred to as patois – hoping to make a real written language of it, with rules of spelling and grammar and its own sparkling vocabulary. On the 21st of May, the seven, known as the seven Félibres, founded an association, the Félibrige, choosing a seven-pointed star as their emblem. The popular success of *Mirèio*, a long poem in twelve cantos, earned the Provençal tongue recognition as a literary language, and conferred renown on Mistral's native village, Maillane, as the etymological birthplace of this poetic tongue. Here, he wrote *Calendau* and *The Treasure of the Félibrige*, a reference work covering the linguistic and cultural riches of Provence, as well as his epic *Lou Pouèmo dòu Rose – The Song of the Rhone*. A language of subtle nuance and intensity, it lends itself quite naturally to the heady excesses of poetic license, extravagant exaggeration, and outrageously tall stories.

2

THE PROVENCE OF MISTRAL AND DAUDET

CAMARGUE AND ALPILLES

MONTAGNETTE AND GARRIGUES

THE CAMARGUE

Aigues-Mortes

To bear the name of the watery element that once played so important a role in shaping its destiny is not the least remarkable characteristic of this little town, whose name, Aigues-Mortes – meaning dead waters – recalls the days when waves still beat against its walls.

In a landscape where the horizon is no more than a thin line separating the vast sky from level expanses of lagoon and marsh, the high walls of Aigues-Mortes stand as the bold witness to the compelling faith of its founder, Louis IX – the future Saint Louis. Founded by royal commission in 1240, the town was designed as the kingdom's gateway to the Mediterranean, through which France was to reach the shores of the Holy Land, and defend them or be dammed. With its streets laid out in a regular grid, with a rectangular square, Place Saint-Louis, this quadrilateral town is surrounded by high curtain walls. In 1240, to the northwest of the town, work began on the Constance Tower. A solid, cylindrical keep, blind and indestructible, bristling defensively with portcullises, loopholes and embrasures, its simple but uncompromisingly closed design led it, quite naturally, to be used as a prison. The upper rooms, easier to guard, were converted into cells where any real, potential, or presumed enemies of the crown – from monks of the Knights Templars, whose order was quashed by Philip the Fair, to arrogant and insubordinate nobles, and the followers of the heretical and dangerous new Protestant move-

Aigues-Mortes: The ramparts

ment – were left to languish. Among them was that fierce defender of the reformed faith, Mazel, who, with his fellow prisoners, devised so fantastic an escape – with digging noises discretely muffled by fervent psalm singing, a long rope made from pieces of cloth knotted together then lowered to the foot of the tower, and a headlong flight into the depths of the marshes – that it could have come straight from one of Alexandre Dumas' more dramatic novels. Another courageous and unyielding Protestant, Marie Durand, survived thirty terrible years of detention within the walls of Constance Tower.

The high curtain walls that surround the town were built to the rules of 13th century military architecture. The twin round towers of La Gardette Gate still guard the narrow passage through which the road to the hill country runs. Infinite care had to be taken, innumerable difficulties overcome, and great determination applied to build on this sandy, alluvial coastal site, completely devoid of stone. Thousands of tons of rock were brought in from distant quarries in the Alpilles and at Beaucaire, and soon towers and gates sprang up, particularly on the side that faced the greatest danger – the south – where small craft, galleys, and later galleons, lay at anchor in the lagoon, tossed on the waves that beat against the city's walls. An access channel, the Grau Louis, was built to communicate with the open sea. On the southwest corner, La Tour des Bourguignons – the Burgundian Tower – was the setting for one of the more bloody episodes of the Hundred Years' War. Slipping into town at night, the Armagnacs surprised the masters of the town, the Burgundians, as they slept, and massacred so many of them that their corpses had to be stored in the tower and salted to keep them from rotting while awaiting burial.

But gradually, as shifting sands crept slowly in and stifled the town, the *aigue* – that lapping water – disappeared. And today, the pounding waves have retreated to the distant coastline, watched over by Espiguette Lighthouse.

Saint Louis, King of France

Steeped in the pure but demanding faith instilled in him by his mother, Queen Blanche of Castille, Louis IX, the future Saint Louis, felt a heavy sense of duty towards this God who had made him His representative on earth. Charitable, just and pious, Louis possessed all the qualities that might be expected to spring from a deeply rooted faith, and performed many great and good deeds. But he was haunted by the idea that his service to God would never be complete unless he undertook a Crusade. In 1240 he decided to build a port, in French waters, on the Mediterranean coast – Aigues-Mortes. The site he chose was a small, desolate piece of land, which he bought from the monks of the nearby Psalmody Abbey. In 1244, Jerusalem fell to the Sultan of Egypt and, responding to Pope Innocent IV's appeal to the Christians of the West, Louis embarked on the Seventh Crusade. At last he began to realise his long-cherished dream. In 1248, countless heavy-hulled ships began to slip through the Grau Louis Canal to moor in the shadow of the walls of Aigues-Mortes. With flags flying, the fleet set sail, arriving, three weeks later, in Cyprus. The following year, the crusaders took the port of Damietta in lower Egypt. But then, taken prisoner at the battle of al-Mansurah in 1250, Louis was forced, in keeping with the best of chivalrous traditions, to pay a ransom and surrender Damietta in order to regain his liberty. Having left France in the prime of life, Louis returned an old man. In 1270, his mystic obsession drew him once more towards the Holy Land and, once more, he set sail from Aigues-Mortes, this time for Tunisia, where he was to end his days, struck down by the plague, which neither knows nor spares either king or villein.

Saint-Gilles

There are many towns which, built on the legend of a saint's life, have adopted that saint's name as their own, and which, in order to establish their unique identity and to anchor themselves firmly in a particular region, have qualified the saint's name by adding that of their region. Saint-Gilles-du-Gard is one such town. Gilles – who was not yet a saint – lived in Greece in the 8th century, and little suspecting that the voice of God would call him to perform miracles, he probably expected to end his days there in peaceful anonymity. Yielding, however, to divine leading, and entrusting body and soul to a fragile craft, he was guided straight to the Camargue coast. Undaunted at the prospect of a life of solitary retreat, Gilles settled into his hermit's cave. But then, the hunt, bearing down in hot pursuit of a gentle hind, arrived, and with it came the miracle. With wildly beating heart, the desperate hind ran to Gilles for help. And, although the noble lord had already let fly his arrow, Gilles' rapid hand intercepted the deadly shaft in mid flight. A miracle was proclaimed and this hallowed spot was deemed a suitable site for an abbey. When a shrine was built around his tomb, crowds of pilgrims on their long journey to Santiago de Compostela began to stop here to pray to the saint. And the abbey, founded in the 9th century, never ceased to hold pride of place in the heart of the estates of that celebrated family, the Raymonds of Saint-Gilles, Counts of Toulouse.

Today, all that remains of Saint-Gilles abbey church, built in monumental halos around the crypt where the saint's tomb lies, is the outer façade, and the barely uncovered foundations of the chancel. Such was the price extracted by the fanatical violence of the Wars of Religion, when willful and determined acts of destruction left the poor abbey in so pitiful a state of ruin that it was impossible to restore it to its original state. Built to a classic cruciform floor

The Noble Raymonds

In 852, Raymond I and Frédelon founded the dynasty of the Counts of Toulouse. In 936, Raymond III Pons, well pleased with his victory over the invading Hungarians, granted himself the title Duke of Aquitaine. But it was Raymond IV who was the first to bear the name Raymond of Saint-Gilles, and associate it with the title Count of Toulouse. An independent prince, ruling over a vast domain, he was quick to take advantage of the providential events that made Saint Gilles' tomb a centre of pilgrimage in its own right and an unavoidable stopping place on the long route through Provence to Santiago de Compostela. Inspired by the impassioned preaching of Pope Urban II, all Christendom buzzed with excitement as it prepared a military expedition to the Holy Land to deliver the tomb of Christ. As the First Crusade got under way, the Pope himself consecrated the altar of Saint-Gilles' Abbey, and Raymond IV went off to fight, for this life and the next, at the Holy Sepulchre. While he was there, managing to procure a property in the Lebanon befitting his noble person, he became Count of Tripoli. In the 13th century, it was Raymond VI who was to play a leading role in the events of history. Lord of an Albigensian domain, infamous breeding ground of the Cathar heresy, Raymond VI wavered between the doctrines of Catharism and Catholicism while pope and monarch alike, eager to clear up such dangerous ambiguities, urged him to take sides. Suspected of the murder of the papal legate, Pierre de Castelnau, at Saint-Gilles, he was excommunicated. He left his son a blighted inheritance, and in spite of his undoubted qualities, Raymond VII was unable to defend it against the increasingly powerful monarchy.

plan, the former abbey church had three naves crossed by a transverse transept and crowned by a vast chancel and five radiating chapels. The abbey's monastic buildings and cloisters have also disappeared.

Although the abbey church's facade was badly damaged during the Revolution, losing some of its original grandeur when the whole of the upper part was destroyed, it is still a masterpiece of Romanesque architecture. Its three doorways, each crowned with a semicircular arched tympanum, are linked together by sculptured frames that fill every last inch of space between column and pilaster. A long procession of characters, worked in high relief with astonishingly close attention paid to form, volume, and the hang of their clothes, act out incidents from the life of Jesus, with particular emphasis on the events of Holy Week. Bordered by a fabulous bestiary, scene succeeds scene, from the *Adoration of the Magi* through to the last moments of Christ's life, death, and resurrection. Judas, the least faithful of the twelve, and Saint Peter are portrayed as key figures, while the the central tympanum takes up the glorius theme of salvation.

The crypt, which, in the past, was visited by pilgrims on their way to Santiago de Compostela, has lost its original Romanesque decor, and the intersecting ribs radiating from their sculptured keystones are Gothic.

By a stroke of good fortune, the old spiral staircase of the abbey church's northern bell tower has survived. Its volume and structure are of so bold a design that it was used as a reference and model by generations of companions of stonemasons who, in places, even carved their emblems into its blond stone.

Just next to the abbey church there is a Romanesque house, reputed to be the birthplace of Guy Foulque, who, in 1215, became Pope Clement IV. The house has a simple facade, with two rows of gemeled windows. On the second floor, a 13th century fireplace with a semicircular hearth is covered with a semicircular hood.

Saint-Gilles: The spiral staircase tower

Saint-Gilles: Stonemasons' emblems

Saint-Gilles: The abbey church

① *Christ Enthroned in Majesty*

② *Judas' Kiss*

③ *A Centaur*

④ A keystone

Across the Camargue

It is no accident that the word for the Greek uppercase letter, *delta*, with its simple triangular shape, was chosen to describe the mouths of certain rivers, such as the Rhone, which, unfolding and meandering along among the cushioned softness of their overabundant alluvium, open their wide triangular mouths towards the sea. Surrounded by water – by the fresh waters of the Grand Rhone to the east and the Petit Rhone to the west, and by short choppy salt waters, such as those of the Gulf of Saintes-Maries, to the south – the Camargue is more of an island than part of the continent.

A land of sun, wind and water, the Camargue lives in a world of its own. The age-old struggle between land and water takes on so subtle a nature here that what seems at first to be a perfectly static landscape is, in fact, one subject to constant change. Carrying thousands of tons of alluvium in its waters, the Rhone has formed scattered strips of land, called *launes*, where roads are laid, crops are planted, and traditional low farmhouses, or *mas*, are built, more or less on dry ground. Around them, the captive waters spread out into marshes, covered in rustling reeds. Further south, the Mediterranean comes into play, forming compact sandbars whose gentle curves are constantly altered by coastal currents, while wind and sun whip the lagoons' bright waters into choppy waves, or dry them into salt-caked *sansouires*. But what lends this landscape the fragile beauty and early morning innocence of the dawn of creation is the illusive presence of the Camargue's white horses. Secretive and wary, these thoroughbred cousins of the Paleolithic *equus* are broad-backed and solidly built, perfectly adapted to their semiaquatic environment, as are their even hardier companions, the Camargue bulls, highly-strung and fierce, with handsome lyre-shaped horns and ebony coats. Although their wanderings may be restricted by barbed wire, they are, and always

The Camargue: *Gardian* and *manade*

will be, creatures of the wind. And, as if affording a sudden glimpse of paradise, flocks of flamingos, in frilly pink feathered toutous, rise in graceful ballets against the setting sun. More than just a land of limpid beauty, the Camargue is rich in centuries-old traditions. Wading through pale seas of waving grasses, the *gardians*, or Camargue cowboys – so much more than simple cowherds – and their inseparable white mounts, seem to fuse together into single, almost mythological, creatures, half man, half horse. Armed with three-pronged forks, they drive the herds of young bulls, known as *manades*, together for branding. Quickly and cleanly, a notch is cut deftly in the bull's ear, and a red-hot iron applied unflinchingly to his flank. The whole operation, from the time when the outraged beast is hobbled with ropes, to the angry snort it gives as it heaves itself up to freedom, takes only a few brief moments. Traditional Camargue cabins are simple and modest. With whitewashed walls and their roofs, rounded at one end, covered in regular sheaves of long reeds, or *sagno*, they somehow manage to withstand the worst of the mistral's ill-tempered gales.

Although the Camargue is an agricultural area, far from spoiling the region's natural beauty, the tilled lands seem, almost miraculously, to have retained its very essence. Sky-blue paddy fields bristle with tender green tufts while, for five long months, the grain swells with water as it ripens in the sun. Highly mechanised farming methods have made planting out and harvesting routine tasks, and the silky, translucent grains of rice produced here can rival any of their Asiatic counterparts. As the slowly circulating salt-saturated waters of the salt marshes spread out in geometric grids, they gradually evaporate in the sun, leaving behind thick white deposits of salt.

In response to the growing and compelling need to protect this unique and fragile environment, the Parc Naturel Régional du Camargue (Camargue Regional Nature Reserve) was created around Vaccarès Lagoon.

Bullfights and Rosettes

Armed with no more than his finely-tuned reflexes and quick wits, the *razeteur*, or bullfighter, dressed all in white, faces the *lou biou*, the little black bull, in the regular combat known as the *cocarde*. Using his *razet*, or hook, the aim is to snatch the *cocarde*, or rosette, from between the bull's menacing horns, to which it is firmly attached. No blood. No killing. Just a simple game full of the joy and lively generosity of Provence. Released into the arena to the enthusiastic cheers of the excited crowd, the furious bull charges with lowered horns at the maddening white form. Then, it is up to the *razeteur* to decide whether to dodge the charge and leap over the protective barrier, or confront the bull head on, in the hope, one day, of winning that ultimate prize, conferred at Nîmes, of the famous *cocarde d'or* – the golden rosette.

The *razeteur*

❷

1 Eagle owl

2 Spoonbill

3 Harrier eagle

4 Cattle egret

5 Royal kite

The Pont de Gau Bird Sanctuary

The Camargue marshlands, by their very nature, provide both a perfect permanent home for certain sedentary species of bird and an ideal stopping place for many of the great migrators as they journey between northern summer latitudes and warmer winter climes. The tourist information centre at Pont de Gau, on Ginès Lagoon, was created in order to help provide an efficient means of protecting the flora and fauna of this fragile habitat. A variety of well-researched pamphlets, brochures and other literature present an interesting and educational approach to this exceptionally rich environment. A walk along one of the numerous signposted footpaths, through the unspoilt countryside of the bird sanctuary's dozen or more hectares of marshes, brings the visitor into close contact with many protected species. Vast aviaries house the shyer, more elusive birds which would otherwise be difficult to spot. There is no doubt that it is the pink flamingo that rules the roost here. The Latin root of this bird's name, *flamma*, meaning flame, is a reminder that, in the folds of its wings, under the soft outer pale pink feathers, this most elegant of wading birds hides a vivid coral-pink and fire-red livery. The cattle egret, faithful to the *manade* of bulls that gives it board and lodging, feasts on the swarms of parasitic insects that plague the herd. Although shy and retiring by nature, the spoonbill, with its strange long black beak splayed into a wide, flat, bright orange-coloured disk — so practical for rooting about in the teeming mud — rarely goes unnoticed. The Jean-le-Blanc or harrier eagle, somewhere between a hawk and an eagle, the eagle owl, with its tufts of feathers that resemble a cat's ears, and the sternly staring royal kite, are just some of the noble guests of the Pont de Gau Bird Sanctuary.

Pink flamingos

①

②

Saintes-Maries-de-la-Mer

It is only a hundred years or so since Saintes-Maries-de-la-Mer became so inseparably associated with the Gypsies. And yet, recent as the tradition may be, the depth of religious fervour demonstrated as they gather each year, on the 24th of May, around their patron saint, Sarah, commands no uncertain respect. As the pilgrimage ends, the town, just a stone's throw from the Petit Rhone, returns to a quieter way of life. A very ancient chapel is said to have existed here, but opinions on the origin and meaning of its name, *Sancta Maria de Ratis*, vary. *Saint Mary of the Raft*, celebrating the little boat said to have run ashore here with the two Marys in the 1st century, or *Saint Mary of the Isle*, describing this hillock of dry land, surrounded by water and shifting sand banks? But whatever the origin of its name, the town's site is remarkable, and its church, built right on the sea front, watches over it carefully.

This golden church, built to the simplest of architectural designs, is a veritable fortress, with a long nave spiked with buttresses, and an apse in the form of a circular crenellated keep. Only its bell gable, rising well above all danger of attack, has open arcades. Apart from a few sculptured capitals, fringed with a finely chiseled decor of prickly acanthus leaves, the church's interior is very sober. Beneath the apse is the crypt, which was rebuilt during restoration work undertaken by King René. It is here that the statue of Sarah stands, covered in jewels and shining fabrics, and bathed in the light of flickering candle flames. The tower above the apse houses Saint Michael's Chapel and the shrines of the two Saint Marys. It was also the setting chosen by Mistral for the death by sunstroke of his fragile *Mirèio*.

The Folco de Baroncelli Museum, named after its founding *manadier*, houses the many souvenirs he so painstakingly and lovingly collected in order to preserve something of the Camargue herdsmen's traditional way of life.

Saintes-Maries-de-la-Mer: The church - A capital

Saintes-Maries-de-la-Mer: *Sarah*

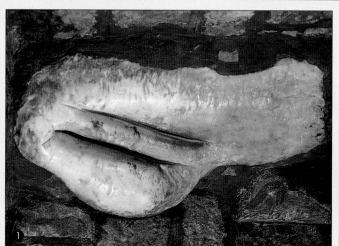

Saintes-Maries-de-la-Mer:

❶ *The Saints' Pillow*

❷ The Gypsy pilgrimage: Banners

❸ The Gypsy pilgrimage: The saints at the blessing by the sea

❹ The Gypsy pilgrimage: *Gardians*

❺ The Gypsy pilgrimage: Saint Sarah

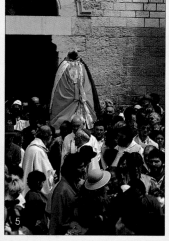

42

Mary, Mary and Sarah

The product of legend and long tradition, the true origins of the pilgrimage to the town of Saintes-Maries-de-la-Mer are somewhat obscure. The use of so common a Christian name in the plural, however, can be explained easily enough. A number of years after the death of Christ, Mary, the mother of James and sister of the Virgin Mary, and Mary, the mother of James and John the disciples, together with Lazarus and his sister Martha, Mary Magdalene, and Maximinus, were abandoned by the Jews of Jerusalem on a fragile skiff, with neither sails nor supplies. Sarah, the old Egyptian servant, insisted on sharing their plight. Trusting their souls to God, they let the boat drift, until, exhausted but alive, they found themselves on a beach just a few kilometres from the mouth of the Petit Rhone. The younger ones set out to evangelise Provence, leaving the two Marys and Sarah, by now too old to travel, near a little oratory. A chapel built over their tomb became known, in the 10th century, as Notre-Dame-de-la-Mer – Our Lady of the Sea. Then, on the 2nd of December, 1448, during work on the chapel's crypt, King René, Count of Provence, discovered what were claimed to be the remains of the saints' relics – two skeletons and a strange polished marble block, scored with two deep grooves, which became known as the *Oreiller des Saintes*, or the *Saints' Pillow*. The chapel was enlarged and embellished, and began to welcome ever growing numbers of pilgrims. In May and October, the saints' relics are carried on a wave of deeply pious fervour to the sea shore, where they are blessed and plunged into the water. The veneration of Sarah as the patron saint of the Gypsies is much more recent, with the earliest records dating only from the last century.

Saintes-Maries-de-la-Mer: *The Saints' Boat*

Arles

At the tip of the triangle formed where the twin branches of the Rhone separate into their delta, a rocky outcrop rises above the level of the plain. The Phocaeans, already well established at *Massalia*, traveled the shifting marshlands and, on this island of dry land, commanding a clear view over the wide river flowing at its feet to the glistening sea beyond the reeds, they founded *Thélinè*. Soon adopting the name *Arlate* – which later became Arles – this marshland town controlled the major route through the Rhone valley from the Gallic inland regions to *Massalia* and the Mediterranean. Like its neighbour and rival, *Massalia*, *Arlate* took sides in the struggle between those two ambitious Romans, Pompey and Caesar. But while *Massalia* supported Pompey, *Arlate*, opportunist, yet prudent, backed Caesar. When *Massalia* fell to Caesar, in 49 B.C., *Arlate* became a military colony and home to the veterans of the VIth Legion. Raised suddenly to the rank of a Roman town, *Arlate* was immediately subjected to a widespread and thoroughly comprehensive programme of urban development. A rectangular, portico-lined **forum** was built over its cryptoporticus – a vaulted basement structure, supported by solid colonnades. Among the ruins of the **theatre**, the delicate silhouette of a pair of columns with sculptured capitals still stands out boldly against the sky – a romantic and timeless reminder of the splendours of the past. The theatre, with three tiers of arcades on its outer wall, could accommodate 10,000 spectators. The alcoves in the stage wall once housed a number of statues, of which the best-known, the *Venus of Arles*, discovered in 1651, was presented to King Louis XIV and displayed at the Louvre. To the west of Hauture Hill, the **amphitheatre** – today known as the Arènes – was built in the 1st century B.C.. It was almost certainly used as the model for the one at Nîmes, which is thought to have been built at a slightly later date. Around the

Arles: The town and the Arènes

oval arena, the *cavea*, which rises in a flight of terraces to the top of the two arcaded storeys of its exterior facades, could hold a crowd of 20,000. Instead of the more usual Roman vault, a flat flagstone pavement laid over the amphitheatre's access galleries bears witness to the Hellenic influence that lasted here throughout ancient times.

Like those of many imposing religious buildings, the origins of **Saint Trophimus' Cathedral** are lost in that strange mixture of fact and fiction that is the very essence of legend. Although he was certainly one of the first bishops of Arles, little else is known of Saint Trophimus himself. The church, built at the dawn of the Middle Ages, was originally dedicated to Saint Stephen. Then, in the 12th century, it recovered the relics of Saint Trophimus, adopted him as its patron saint, and changed its name. The facade's sculptured portal dates from this period and shows how, for a long time, Roman influence remained one of the characteristic features of Provençal Romanesque architecture. With its central door crowned by a barrel vaulted tympanum with concentric arches, framed by a finely colonnaded loggia, the portal has the archaic shape of a Roman triumphal arch. At the centre of the composition, Christ, enthroned in majesty with two fingers raised, delivers his verdict. A bull, a lion, an eagle and a young man, all with long angelic wings, represent the four gospel writers, Luke, Mark, John and Matthew. The traditional scene of the *Final Judgement*, the ultimate preoccupation of all Christians concerned with the salvation of their souls, unfolds beneath the unblinking gaze of apostles and patriarchs. Haloed in heavenly glory, they watch as the good, the wise and the elect advance on their right, while the chastened damned are led away in chains towards the gates of hell. Neatly lined up between the fine columns of the loggia, the stern figures of the great saints, among them Saint Bartholomew, Saint James the Lesser, Saint John and Saint Peter, complete the scene. Like a picture book

The Réattu Museum

After the French Revolution, Jacques Réattu, a painter from Arles, bought and restored the 15th century former priory of the Order of the Knights of Malta, making it into a museum. Several of the museum's rooms are dedicated to his work. Its main vocation, however, was to provide a prestigious showcase for those painters and sculptors whose work is representative of modern and contemporary art. Hanging next to the works of local artists like Raspal, Réattu's uncle, and Rousseau, the famous Camargue painter, are those of artists whose fame reaches far beyond Provence's borders: Gauguin, Vasarely, Dufy, Léger and, in a different vein, Zadkine, César and Toni Grand. Always fond of Arles, Picasso, as a venerable old man with that characteristic glint of mischief in his eye, gave the town a collection of fifty seven drawings, made, in a matter of weeks, at the beginning of 1971.

Arles: The Réattu Museum - A sketch by Picasso

Vincent Van Gogh:

❶ *The Alyscamps*

❷ *The Woman of Arles*

❸ *The Arènes at Arles*

❹ *Self-Portrait with Amputated Ear*

Vincent Van Gogh

No artist, least of all Van Gogh, could be left indifferent by the unique luminous quality of the skies of Arles. Tormented and troubled, Van Gogh dedicated much of his life to helping those in greater misery than himself, and his desolate wanderings in the poor quarters of Europe's great industrial cities drove him, with an almost fanatical zeal, to a euphoric state of self-denial. Later, it was painting that was to provide him with the impetus to continue his all-consuming quest after the Absolute and give him reason to live. Coming to Provence, he discovered a new quality of light that at once began to flood his work. Although the intense luminosity of his deep blues, golden yellows and absolute blacks may seem to imply that his obsessive passion and despair had given way to harmony and peace of mind, the spasmodic violence of his brushstrokes, which make the thick paint of his suns crackle and the tousled heads of his sunflowers burst with life, reveal the torment that still haunted him. He worked ceaselessly during his stay in Provence, becoming, in his own words, a "painting machine". He painted any number of subjects, creating as many masterpieces: the boats on the beach of Saintes-Maries-de-la-Mer, the bridge at Langlois, the woman of Arles, the Alyscamps with their cypress trees, golden fields, sunflowers, olive trees twisting in the wind, fabulous irises filling the ditches near Saint-Rémy-de-Provence, and even the simple decor of his little bedroom in Arles, painted in the most contrasting of shades. But eventually, madness was to send him reeling into the dark realms of confusion, driving him to the asylum of Saint-Paul-de-Mausole, to self-mutilation, and finally to suicide – a tragic end to the artist's life, dissipating, like a last explosion of colour on canvas, into a thousand golden brushstrokes.

The cloisters at Saint-Paul-de-Mausole, near Saint-Rémy-de-Provence

chiseled out of stone, the scenes depict the barely disguised promises and threats that were to be carefully considered by all good Christians. The high, narrow, barrel vaulted nave leads to a most exuberantly decorated Gothic chancel which still houses the sculpted sarcophagi of the founding saints of the Christian doctrine, as well as some Aubusson tapestries. A stroll through the cool arcades of the **cloisters**, overshadowed by Saint Trophimus' square bell tower, is a must. The north and east galleries, dating from the 12th century, boast a rich Romanesque decoration which is both naive and full of symbolism. On the corner pillars, crowded with statues whose long robes fall in rigid pleats, bas-reliefs illustrate the moving theme of the stoning of Saint Stephen, and show the Holy women, each carrying a little flask of perfume.

The **Place de la République** provides a brief summary of the many and varied aspects of the town's long history, bearing the characteristic traces left by each period's architecture

Saint Trophimus': Detail of a Christian sarcophagus

Saint Trophimus': The cloisters - *Saint Andrew*

Saint Trophimus': *The Stoning of Saint Stephen*

and beliefs. The Egyptian granite obelisk that soars skywards once graced Arles' Roman amphitheatre. In 1675, it was incorporated into a monumental fountain and raised on a pedestal decorated with bronze lions.

The **Hotel de Ville**, or Town Hall, was rebuilt in the 17th century, when its hall was adorned with a vaulted ceiling whose design makes it a masterpiece of interlocking shapes and volumes. Rising over the rooftops, the clock tower was modeled on the famous *tholos* of Glanum mausoleum. In keeping with ancient Roman tradition, the sarcophagi of the town's dignitaries were lined up at the entrance to the town, under the shady canopies of the *Via Aurelia*. Far from disappearing with the spread of Christianity, the **Alyscamps** – whose name gives the modern *Champs-Elysées* – took on an increasingly important character, becoming one of the most celebrated necropolises of the Christian world. Bordered with time-ravaged sarcophagi, the long alley leads to **Saint Honorat's Church**, with its openwork bell tower.

Arles: Saint Honorat's Church

The Museum of Christian Art

The Museum of Christian Art, located in what used to be the Jesuit chapel, houses a large number of fine marble Paleo-Christian sarcophagi from the 4th century. Their sculptured facades are covered in delicate friezes that depict hunting scenes, Adam and Eve politely getting to know each other in paradise, and events from the life of Jesus, every detail represented with meticulous care. Taken from Arles' two Paleo-Christian necropolises, Saint-Genest and the Alyscamps, they demonstrate just how much Christianity benefited from the conversion of the Roman emperors in the 4th century. Scenes from the Bible pay a sophisticated tribute to both prophets and saints. Christ washing Peter's feet, Daniel in the lion's den, and the sarcophagus of the heavenly spouses, with its three sculptured registers and central imago, all bear witness to the religious zeal of the faithful.

Museum of Christian Art: Sarcophagus with imago

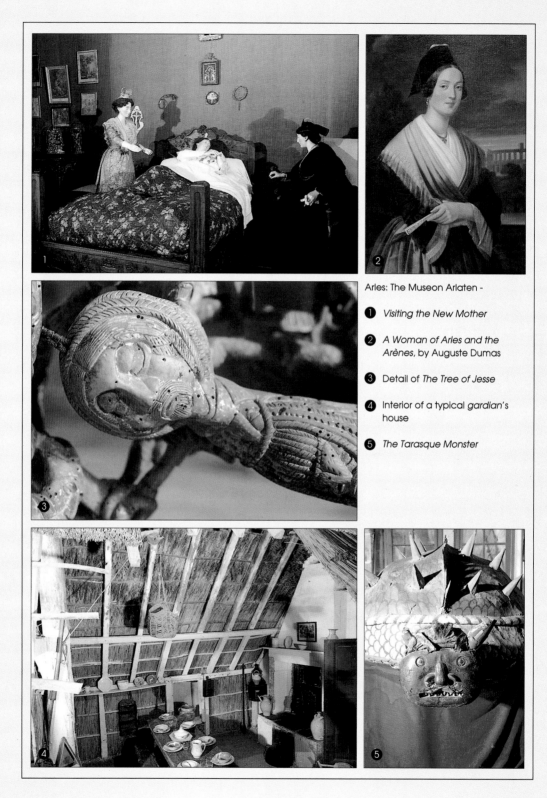

Arles: The Museon Arlaten -

1 *Visiting the New Mother*

2 *A Woman of Arles and the Arènes,* by Auguste Dumas

3 Detail of *The Tree of Jesse*

4 Interior of a typical *gardian's* house

5 *The Tarasque Monster*

The "Museon Arlaten"

Housed within the walls of the Hôtel de Laval-Castellane, a palatial 16th century town house, the Museon Arlaten (*museon* means museum) was conceived, designed and built by Provence's famous poet, Mistral. In celebration of his Nobel Prize for Literature, he intended the museum as a tribute to Provence's generous ethnographic heritage, a storehouse of all its traditions and folklore. Fearing that the region's distinctive identity, however strong it might be, would be eroded, if not wiped out altogether, by the virtually irresistible movement towards uniformity that was sweeping through France, Mistral's driving ambition was to protect Provence's language – already in a state of decline and already no more than the dwindling reserve of the privileged older generation – from that synonym of modernity, the French language. His desire was to ensure that the superb traditional costume, with its perfect blend of natural grace and meticulous sophistication, and the art of hairdressing – more a form of living sculpture than a simple hairstyle – would live on. And he wanted to preserve every detail of the legend in which the evil, red, green and bloodthirsty Tarasque monster became miraculously docile when faced with the determined Saint Martha. To these ends, Mistral collected the smallest mementos of everyday life, from the tools of diverse trades and skills, to wonderfully fragile spun glass religious scenes. For the delight of future generations, he reconstituted a number of traditional interiors, such as the cosy kitchen of a Provençal *mas* on Christmas Eve, or the delivery room with its cot covered in starched lace. And no visit is complete without pausing to study the charming little labels on which Mistral himself recorded, in his fine poet's hand, all the rich details of the land of *Mirèio*.

Arles: The Museon Arlaten - The Calendale Room

①

②

Montmajour Abbey

In the middle of the vast watery plains where tender young rice plants rustle in the breeze, a rocky island suddenly emerges. This solid ridge, so rare and so firm a foothold in the heart of this impenetrable marshland, has been inhabited by man for centuries past. It was in the 10th century that a community of monks founded Montmajour Abbey here. Enterprising and hardworking, they undertook the immense task of draining the surrounding marshes, digging ditches and channels to dry out the wide plain stretching down to the Rhone. Gifts of property and the Festival of Forgiveness, instituted in 1030, raised the funds needed to transform the abbey into one of Provence's greatest religious centres. But such wealth soon attracted the attention of greedy outsiders, and, in the 14th century, the abbey fell into commendam. Taxed by abbots whose sole purpose was, at best, to drain off as much of its huge income as

possible, the abbey fell into decline, its spiritual force exhausted. Closed by order of Louis XVI, it was later confiscated by the revolutionary government and sold off to the highest bidder. Dismembered and disfigured, it seemed destined to become no more than a stone quarry until the state, taking pity on its majestic ruins, redeemed and restored it. The unfinished 12th century abbey church of Notre-Dame was built over a lower church – a crypt – half exposed to the open air, half buried underground, with a remarkably well-proportioned barrel vaulted and domed ceiling. The arches that support the cloisters' semicircular vaulted ceiling rest on brackets chiseled into hideous monsters and leering faces. The Abbot's Tower, a massive crenellated 14th century keep, overshadows Saint Peter's Chapel, which clings to its rock, a reminder of the abbey's early days, while, outside the abbey church's walls, the Holy Cross (Sainte-Croix) Chapel still watches over the ancient tombs of the Paleo-Christian necropolis.

Montmajour Abbey: Saint Peter's Chapel

Montmajour Abbey: The crypt

Montmajour Abbey: Fabulous animal heads

2

THE ALPILLES

Over the Hills...

Their name may echo that of the great mountains beyond the Durance, but the Alpilles lay no pretentious claims to equality with the Alps, even if their harsh and splendid landscape – with chiseled peaks and scorched ravines heady with the scent of rosemary and thyme, rockslides of white boulders and complex labyrinths of caves – is quite in keeping with the best of all Mediterranean traditions.

In the 3rd century, the water supplied by **Barbegal Roman Aqueduct** was used to organise milling on what can only be described as an industrial scale. Released from a reservoir on higher ground, it powered the paddle wheels of a series of mills set at intervals along its course. The mathematics of the operation were simple: multiplying the number of mills naturally multiplied flour production by as much. In Roman times, a second aqueduct supplied the town of Arles, just ten kilometres away.

Home of the poet Charloun Rieu, the village of **Paradou** nestles among the olive groves that stretch out at the foot of the Alpilles.

The village of **Eyguières** is located where the Alpilles come down to meet the Crau Plain. Water is abundant here, and it spills, murmuring, in long trickles from many fountains, such as the Coquille, or Shell, Fountain.

In the Deffends Hills, overlooking the village of Lamanon, **Calès Caves** were dug into troglodytic dwellings by the anxious populations that lived here from Neolithic times until the Middle Ages. All approaches were defended, and the silos, cut into the very heart of the rock and used to store the community's precious reserves of grain, were jealously guarded. From this vantage point, the view stretches into the distance, as far as Berre Lagoon.

Paradou's "Petite Provence"

It seems only natural that here, in the home of the *santon*, there should be a permanent exhibition of the works of Provence's greatest master *santon* makers. And here, in Paradou's "Petite Provence", nearly three hundred of these minutely detailed figures, worked on a scale of 1:6, illustrate the daily life and traditions of 18th and 19th century Provence, with the café on the town square, the game of *pétanque* beneath the plane trees, and the church with its central oculus and flight of steps, not to mention the colourful vegetable and flower market. In all, eight thousand hours of painstaking work, and not a minute of it wasted!

Petite Provence: *The Town Square*

Petite Provence: *Grape-Harvesting Time*

In the 14th century, the **Castellas de Roquemartine**, Roquemartine Castle, perched high on its rocky platform, became the lair of the bands of mercenaries in the pay of the terrible Lord of Les Baux, Raymond de Turenne.

Close to **Eygalières**, there is a Romanesque chapel dedicated to Saint Sixtus. Framed between dark cypress trees and outlined against a deep indigo blue sky, the scene is a perfect example of the charm and subtle beauty of a typical Provençal landscape.

At the foot of the range, opposite the Tarascon Plain which stretches as far as the Rhone, **Saint Gabriel's Chapel** keeps watch at an ancient crossroads, several thousands of years old. Today, all that remains of the old Gallo-Roman town of *Ernaginum* are some half-buried ruins, although its streets and the surrounding marshes must once have buzzed with the flourishing activity of a rich and busy trading centre. As the moving sight of their lowly tombs bears witness, an early Christian community was established here. In the 12th century, Saint

Gabriel's Chapel was built here, on the site of an earlier building, of which no trace now remains. The striking simplicity of its architectural design and the modesty of its decor are truly remarkable. The chapel's facade is hollowed out in simple geometric shapes, from its barrel vaulted tympanum to its triangular pediment decorated with naive sculptures of the expressionless figures typical of the early days of Christian art. And above, edged by a ring of stone, is the perfect round of its oculus, with, at each point of the compass, images of a lion, a bull, a young man and an eagle, the traditional symbols used to represent the four gospel writers, Mark, Luke, Matthew and John. The nave is very simple, with a barrel vaulted ceiling and a cul-de-four apse. As the marshes gradually disappeared, the town fell into decline, and the keep was left stranded on its hilltop, no longer able to fulfill its role of strategic stronghold. Only the chapel remains, an incongruous sentinel guarding ancient paths that have long since become major highways.

Saint Gabriel's Chapel

Saint Gabriel's Chapel: Detail of the tympanum

Saint Gabriel's Chapel: Detail of the tympanum

②

Fontvieille Windmill

The squat silhouette of *Daudet's Mill*, with its sails spread wide against a violet sky, is a familiar part of every French childhood. Just a climb to the top of the hill brings it all flooding back: turning the pages of the old book, edging a hesitant little finger along the line, tripping and stumbling over words that were to remain, forever, engraved on some small corner of childhood memory. Exposed to the elements, gently caressed and violently buffeted in turn, the mill knows all thirty-two of Provence's winds, from *damo* to *souleu*, by name. Its ancient timber frame still houses the ingenious works of its great oak and boxwood cogwheels. How strange that this ordinary little windmill, which came to represent Daudet's idyllic retreat, and which still has that simple, good-natured air to be found in the *Letters* that made it famous, should be thrust into the noble ranks of France's great historic monuments!

Alphonse Daudet

Born in Nîmes in 1840, Alphonse Daudet studied in Lyon before moving to Paris, returning to Provence only in 1864, to stay with friends, the Ambroy family, owners of Montauban Castle, near Arles. Here, in the hills of Fontvieille, he found inspiration and discovered the vividly picturesque subject matter for his writings. But Daudet lived and worked in Montauban, and the Moulin Saint-Pierre, now known as *Daudet's Mill*, never actually belonged to him. His works, including Le *Petit Chose*, L'*Arlésienne*, and the famous *Lettres de Mon Moulin*, have earned him acclaim as one of France's greatest 19th century writers. And the heroes of his books, such as the colourful Master Cornillius, Mr. Seguin and the Rev. Gaucher, are so extraordinarily lifelike that it is easy to forget they are not real people.

Fontvielle: Daudet's Mill - Detail of the cogwheel mechanism

Les Baux-de-Provence

A long, narrow limestone butte with abruptly steep and jagged sides is a safe place to settle in, and the people that occupied this unassailable site, taking full advantage of its natural strength, were quick to impose their rule over the plains of Provence. In the Middle Ages, when the noble Lords of Les Baux established their eagles' nest of a stronghold on this rocky needle, Mistral coined that well-known phrase that so aptly described them: "Race d'aiglons, jamais vassale" – "Race of eagles, vassals never". Proud, vain and arrogant, the Lords of Les Baux set about establishing the most staggering of family trees, whose roots, far from being lost in the muddy obscurity of time, reached down as far as the legendary figure of Balthazar, the Magi king. In his honour, they added a shining star of Bethlehem to their dynasty's coat of arms, together with the strange, rather fatalistic, and not very Catholic, motto

"Au hazard Balthazar" – "As you will, Balthazar!". In the 11th century, shaking off the burdensome tutelage of feudal hierarchy, the Lords of Les Baux refused any allegiance with either the Counts of Provence or Barcelona. From the safety of their solid fortress on the rocks of Les Baux, they ruled over seventy-nine towns and villages, from the Durance to the Var. Their political ambitions, however, went beyond the limits of their physical strength and, at the beginning of the 13th century, they lost their claim to the title of Counts of Provence to their rivals, the Counts of Catalonia. Under this long line of belligerent and hotheaded Lords, Provence was the stage for many bloody conflicts. But when Raymond de Turenne, guardian of the young Alix des Baux, came onto the scene in the late 14th century, the violence and terror reached new heights. Known as the *Fléau de la Provence* – the Curse of Provence – and proud of it, he fed his insatiable appetite for power with cruel acts of pillage and massacre.

Les Baux-de-Provence: The Columbarium

But Les Baux has another, far sweeter, claim to fame as the seat of the sumptuous courts of love, where troubadours would pit their wits against one another in songs of praise to the court's most beautiful ladies. And indeed, the memory of those ladies lives on: Azalaïs, Passerose, Phanette, Doulce and Clairette, dressed in garlands of roses and diaphanous veils, the muses of that *fyne amor*, that exquisite art of courtly lovemaking so highly prized in these southern courts.

Established as a barony under the Counts of Provence, Les Baux at last found peace and prosperity under the influence of Countess Jeanne of Provence. At the end of the 15th century, Les Baux became part of the kingdom of France, but the memory of the legendary rebelliousness of the Lords of Les Baux was still fresh in the minds of the French monarchy, who in 1633, found sufficient pretext to have the citadel demolished. Becoming a marquessate, Les Baux was entrusted to the protective rule of the Princes of Monaco, the Grimaldi family. In 1791, the town became a commune of France. Impoverished, destroyed, and finally deserted, the fortress became little more than a pile of toppled stones, abandoned to sun and wind, until, moved by the sight of its ruins, and unwilling to let the memory of such past glory fade into oblivion, Mistral and Daudet combined their considerable talent and zeal to undertake its defence.

Today, all that remains of the partly troglodytic castle are the haughty ruins of its keep. The nearby chapel once lay within the castle walls, as did the dovecote – the symbol of the power and prestige of the castle's Lords – hewn into the very rock face and riddled with thousands of niches. Standing on the edge of the cliff, Saracen Tower and Paravelle Tower were once part of a system of curtain walls, long since disappeared. At the point of the spur there is a monument to Charloun Rieu, Les Baux's native poet, songwriter, and author of a Provençal translation of *The Odyssey*. The village of Les Baux has been extensively restored, and

Les Baux-de-Provence: The Charloun Rieu Monument

Les Baux-de-Provence:

1. Place Saint-Vincent

2. Queen Jeanne's Pavilion

3. The White Penitent's (Pénitents-Blancs) Chapel

4. The quarries in the Val d'Enfer

5. The bas-relief of the Trémaïé

much of the Renaissance charm of the Man-ville and Jean de Brion mansions has been re-covered. Flanked by a campanile, the 12th century Saint Vincent's Church is the setting for the *Pastrage* Festival, a Christmas celebration of the shepherds' adoration of the newborn Christ. The White Penitents' Chapel is decorated in naive frescos by Yves Brayer.

The closed world of Les Baux opened through a single gate, Porte d'Eyguières – the Water Gate – onto its neighbouring valleys. The gentle *Vallon de la Fontaine* (Valley of the Spring) was chosen, in 1581, by Jeanne de Quiqueran, wife of the Lord of Les Baux, as the site for a lovely Renaissance style garden pavilion, known as Queen Jeanne's Pavilion. The *Val d'Enfer* (Hell Valley), in contrast, is wild, rugged and chaotic. The jagged openings of its underground fossil quarries were used as the setting for Jean Cocteau's film *Orpheus*.

Near the Col de la Vayède (Vayède Pass), Gallo-Roman monuments are decorated in bas-relief images of the Trémaïé and the Gaïè.

The Hôtel de Manville

Lou Santoun - The Little Saint

A few grammes of clay dried in a plaster mold, a palette of bright colours, and a vivid imagination were all that J.-L. Lagnel needed, at the end of the 18th century, to create his popular figurines, the *santouns*, or little saints, known, in modern French, as *santons*. Around the infant Jesus, all pink and wriggly on his bed of straw, an animated but immobile crowd gathers in a simple expression of enthusiastic piety. There is the *pastre*, or shepherd, the *tambourinaïre*, or tambourine player, the miller with his sack of flour, the *amoulaïre*, or knife grinder, the fishmonger with his hands on his hips, the *boufarèu*, or fat-cheeked angel who *buffes* into his trumpet, and *lou ravi*, the simpleton, his head in the clouds. Indeed, the whole of Provence is there, thronging the paths to the Holy Crib.

The Santon Museum: *A Provençal Woman*

①

②

Glanum

More than a thousand years before the birth of Christ, the Ligurians chose to settle in the place where the ancient route that winds through the Alpilles emerges onto the plain, a site which afforded them the double advantage of control over the pass and access to the riches of the plain that stretched northwards before them. The site of Glanum was well chosen and it remained occupied until the untimely, if inevitable, arrival of the barbarian tribes, in the second half of the 3rd century, who put the local population to flight.

Clustered around Saint Remigius' (Saint Rémy's) Church, the newcomers founded a busy and prosperous town, and the ruins of Glanum were left to slip quietly into oblivion. Saint-Rémy-de-Provence made its fortune from the madder plant, which yields a brilliant crimson dye, and the thistle, used to brush fabric to velvety softness. Today, these ancient industries have given way to horticulture and tourism.

By the time the barbarians had finished with it, all that was left of Glanum was a vast field of ruins and, rather incongruously, two magnificent, well-preserved Roman monuments, known as the *Antiques*: a commemorative arch and a mausoleum. The old town, lying in the shadow of the steep limestone slopes of Mount Gaussier, nestles among the huge piles of scree accumulated at the foot of the Alpilles. Situated on a seam of soft rock whose ancient quarries provided all the building blocks of its sophisticated thousand year-old architectural heritage, Glanum became known as the city of stone. Extracting and cutting the heavy blocks became a major industry, and the marks left on the stones by the masons' tools provides a valuable insight into the techniques they used.

Glanum's gushing spring – worshipped as a protective god and credited with miraculous healing powers – was central to the development of the site which was occupied continuously from the first millennium B.C. to the Hellenic era, and from the civilised days of the Emperor Augustus to the first cataclysmic invasions of the barbarian tribes.

A shrine, dedicated to the local gods of the Mères and Glan, was built near the source, and around it, a small town grew up under the distant Phocaean influence exerted by Greek Marseilles. Unfortunately, much of the architectural legacy of those far-off times has since disappeared or been reused in later buildings.

Spreading out from the market place, or *agora*, the town boasts a number of fine public buildings, such as the twin temples with their pair of cross-legged heroes, the *bouleuterion*, or council chamber, and a monumental sanctuary surrounded by terraces, with a deep well and a *dromos*, or walkway, closed over with paving stones. Then there are the ornately decorated private houses, such as the Maison des Antes, built in a square around a central porticoed courtyard, and deriving its name from its elegantly pilastered hallway, or *antas*.

After the sudden, destructive arrival of the Romans, it was not until it was raised to the rank of *oppidum latinum*, or provincial town, in about 45 B.C., that Glanum regained something of its earlier splendour. A series of modest, but already ornate, houses gave way to the monuments typical of any Roman town: a forum, a basilica, and the baths, built to the classical plan of a central *palaestra* (gymnasium), surrounded by the *frigidarium, tepidarium* and *caldarium* (cold, warm and hot rooms respectively), heated by the *hypocaust* underground central heating system.

A fortified gate from the Hellenic period, with a zigzag passageway and cart gate, opens onto the ramparts that protect the oldest of Glanum's sanctuaries, the nymphaeum, which houses the town's healing water source. Nearby, a number of fluted columns in the temple dedicated to *Valetudo*, the goddess of health, still stand, and the temple's pool is still fed by the spring. The old paved drain that crosses Glanum, known as the covered canal, was once the town's main thoroughfare.

Beyond this expanse of ruins is the mausoleum, which was not a tomb, but a monument to the memory of the *Julii* family, a local family whose members became Roman citizens. The bas-reliefs on its four faces represent battle scenes while, under the crowning tholos, a pair a toga-clad statues attest to the prestige and status associated with acquiring Roman citizenship.

In contrast to this, the Glanum arch, far from commemorating the integration of the indigenous population, demonstrates another, rather different, aspect of Romanisation, with a very clear illustration of captive Gauls chained to the spoils of war. Its barrel vaulted arcade is decorated with garlands of fruit and leaves, with a very fine hexagonal coffered ceiling.

The Hôtel de Sade, in **Saint-Rémy-de-Provence**, houses a collection of stone treasures gathered from the Glanum site, and contains many of the finds unearthed by Henri Rolland during the numerous archeological digs he undertook there.

Glanum: The Antiques, the arch - *Group of Captives*

Saint-Rémy-de-Provence: Hôtel de Sade - Bas-Relief

Saint-Rémy-de-Provence: Hôtel de Sade - *The Prisoner*

Saint-Rémy-de-Provence: Hôtel de Sade - *Octavia*

❶

❷

3

THE MONTAGNETTE HILLS

Tarascon and Beaucaire

At the point where the lands of Provence, spreading east of the Rhone, once faced the kingdom of France across the river's raging flood, Tarascon Castle still clings to its battered rock opposite its imposing twin and rival, Beaucaire Castle. **Tarascon** Castle was the main and much-loved residence of those Lords of princely lineage, the Counts of Provence, among whose numbers some very famous figures are to be counted. In 1401, Louis II of Anjou commissioned the restoration of what had once been a military construction, dating from the 11th century. From then on, the family's affection for the place never waned, and, as one Count of Provence succeeded another, each left his mark on the castle's architecture and interior decoration. It was Louis II's son, the famous King René, who completed the work begun by his forebears,very tastefully transforming the interior of the fortress into a veritable Renaissance palace.

The medieval castle's stark, inaccessible keep, with its monumental entrance, still remains. Opening out behind the keep, and in striking contrast to it, is the delightful main courtyard, where an airy and delicate spiral staircase climbs to an open loggia. The intricate lacy stonework of the porch that leads to the lower chapel is a masterpiece of Flamboyant Gothic work, and a fine stone balustrade borders the lowered opening to the cantors' chapel. The interior rooms, such as the Council Chamber, are decorated with ancient paintings and have rib vaulted ceilings, while the terrace offers a panoramic view over the Rhone valley.

Although Saint Martha's collegiate church has been extensively restored, its south door is still distinctively Romanesque in style, even if the tympanum's sculptures took a thorough beating in 1793. Saint Martha is Tarascon's patron saint. Legend tells how, armed only with her unshakable faith, Martha fearlessly confronted the Tarasque monster, a hideous creature, with a livid head and a greenish rump bristling with blood-red spines, which, emerging from the waters of the Rhone, would devour both man and beast alike. Smitten by a simple sign of the cross, and instantly transformed into the most docile of animals, it was processed nightly through the town to ward off evil spirits.

But Tarascon is also the home of that colourful character, Tartarin, so vividly brought to life by Daudet's pen. Rather smug, slightly ridiculous, long-winded and pretentious, but also, soft-hearted, generous, and so very human, it is difficult not to identify with him just a little.

Tarascon: Saint Martha's Collegiate Church

In the 17th century, exotic printed cottons imported from the Indies were all the rage in France. In 1938, Charles Deméry revived the fashion, and founded the Souleïado company to export Provence's traditional colourful fabrics all over the world.

Set among winding pathways in the middle of gently rolling grounds, **Beaucaire** Castle – or at least what remains of it after Richelieu's campaign of destruction designed to weaken the power of the great noble families and break up their strongholds – stands on the edge of a terrace overlooking the Rhone. A sharp-edged triangular tower and its fat round companion have both weathered the trials of time and are, together with the curtain walls that run between them, the proud remains of the old royal stronghold that once stood guard over that valuable trading route – the Rhone. Keeping a wary eye on Tarascon and its menacing fortress, Beaucaire Castle concentrated the rest of its attention on the noise and colour of the town's great annual fair, as, each July, all the world's riches crowded into its streets and along its river banks. But, as trade dwindled, Beaucaire, no longer able to indulge in these weeks of festivities, fell into decline.

Although extensively restored in the 18th century, the quaintly named church of Notre-Dame-des-Pommiers – Our Lady of the Apple Trees – still boasts a long sculptured frieze. Like a finely worked piece of embroidery, it depicts major events from the life of Christ, and, in particular, the Last Supper, where the cloth spread over the laden table hangs in delicate folds before the gathered guests. Outside the town there is a 15th century oratory known as the Croix-Couverte, or Covered Cross.

Although the former **abbey of Saint-Roman-de-l'Aiguille** has lain abandoned since the 16th century, it still boasts a 12th century abbot's throne and the moving sight of lines of tombs cut into the very rock. Formerly governed by the Abbot of Saint-Roman, the Romanesque chapel of Saint-Laurent, at nearby **Jonquières**, has a fine semicircular chevet.

Printed Sunshine

In the 17th century, bulging bales of printed cotton fabrics, carried on swaying caravans of camels, came from the distant Indies, through the countries of the Levant, and on to France, via Marseilles. Trade in this exotic and finely coloured printed cloth was lucrative, but variable, so Marseilles, along with the rest of Provence, set about producing its own locally printed materials. The master drapers, however, worried by what they considered as unfair competition to their trade in Indian cottons, persuaded the authorities, under Colbert and, more especially, Louvois, to put a stop to their production. But, as is often the case, prohibition only gave rise to a flourishing black market, and the Provençal percale cottons with their repetitive printed patterns lost none of their appeal. Later, in the 19th century, it was the Provençal workshops that were, in turn, to succumb to growing competitive pressure exerted by the major textile manufacturers. It was not until 1938 that Charles Deméry took up the challenge of restoring Provence's printed cotton industry to its former glory. In Tarascon, the Charles Deméry Museum tells the fascinating story of this ancient tradition, full of the sunshine and colour of Provence.

The Charles Deméry Museum: Dyes and fabrics

Beaucaire and its region:

1. Notre-Dame-des-Pommiers: The freize

2. Saint-Roman-de-l'Aiguille Abbey: Tombs in the rock

3. The Covered Cross

4. Saint-Roman-de-l'Aiguille Abbey: The abbot's throne

5. Jonquières: Saint Lawrence's Chapel

Saint-Michel-de-Frigolet

The first official and authenticated mention of the existence of an abbey at Saint-Michel-de-Frigolet dates from 1133, when the Viscounts of Boulbon donated some fifty hectares of land to what was then Saint Michael's Church. In those days, a community of regular canons, members of the Premonstratensians, lived there by the strict monastic rule of Saint Augustine. Today, all that has survived of the medieval priory is its sturdily solid cloisters, with surbased arcatures, where heavy pillars still support the open barrel vaulted bays.

The long exterior of Saint Michael's Church is truly delightful in its simplicity. An openwork frieze runs along the roof, which has two regular planes, to the tiny bell tower. In the 17th century, two rooms were built on the south side of the cloisters: the chapter house, which served as the monks' meeting place, and the Provençal Room, where, in honour of that legendary and literary figure, the Reverend Father Gaucher, pride of place is given to a still. Records show that the 11th century chapel of Notre-Dame-de-Bon-Remède – Our Lady of the Goodly Cure – was a place of pilgrimage even before Frigolet Abbey was founded. Rebuilt and restored, in the 19th century the chapel finally became part of the new abbey church. It boasts a 17th century, finely gilded, wooden baroque altarpiece which frames twelve paintings of the Mignard school. On the front of the altar, a leather panel, worked in relief using a *repoussé* technique, depicts a fresh-faced, rosy-cheeked Virgin Mary, head wrapped in a dark veil, and eyes modestly lowered, amid a profusion of leafy arabesques. Framed between a pair of wreathed columns, a 17th or 18th century stone statue, probably from the Péru workshops in Avignon, shows a pensive Virgin Mary, wrapped in a sumptuously heavy cloak and holding the Infant Jesus in her arms, their contemplative faces haloed in a golden scallop shell.

The Reverend Father Gaucher's Elixir

"The parish priest of Graveson poured me a draft of a warm, golden green, sparklingly exquisite liqueur, ... and my whole being was filled with sunshine". Alphonse Daudet had just discovered Father Gaucher's elixir. Made by the monks of Saint-Michel-de-Frigolet, this pearly liquid, glinting gold and emerald green, and so much more than a simple liqueur, well deserves the highly prized title of elixir – conferred on only the most mysterious, most divine of beverages. Five or six different herbs gathered in the Alpilles, a large bubbling still to capture the very essence of Provence, and a certain, almost intuitive, dexterity – such are the ingredients needed to produce this heady brew, although some say the recipe itself is closer to some kind of mystic, even slightly diabolical, alchemy, than the kind of tradition that can be learnt in grandma's kitchen. Daudet went on, with perhaps ust of hint of irreverence, to tell the tale of that simple-minded lay brother, Brother Gaucher, who, despite his dull wits, clearly remembered his old Aunt Bégon, and how, as a child, he would roam the scrublands of Provence with her, and watch as she heated, distilled, and brewed the liqueur in her copper cauldrons. His fellow brothers were quick to grasp the potential benefits to be accrued from this terrible potion, but were at a loss to resolve the dreadful dilemma before them: eternal damnation earned in the elixir's heady golden fumes, or the financial ruin of the Abbey. The Prior, a master of rationalisation, is said to have reconciled the conflict by conferring the title of "Reverend Father" on the poor brother, with the words, "Brew, Brother, brew. And we shall grant you, by our prayers, absolution even while you are yet sinning".

4

THE GARRIGUES

Nîmes

With a name as controversial as *Colonia Augusta Nemausus*, there are bound to be a number of theories concerning the origins of Nîmes, capital of the Celtic tribes of the Volcae Arecomici. The first, and least contested, hypothesis traces the beginnings of the city to those ancient days when the *Nemausus* Spring was worshipped as a local god and protector of the town. The spring gave its name to the town and, in the 18th century, the **Jardin de la Fontaine** – the Spring Garden – was built around it. The second theory, which places the emphasis on the word *Augusta*, suggests that Nîmes enjoyed a privileged relationship with the first, if not the best known, Roman emperor,

Octavian Augustus. This claim is based on the fact that a number of Nîmes' monuments and buildings date from the Augustinian period. Indeed, the fortified walls and monumental gates which surround Nîmes, so clearly setting the city limits, were offered as a gift to the urban community by Augustus himself, complete with the **Porte d'Auguste**, which opened onto the Roman road to Arles, and the colossal tower, **Tour Magne**, set on the hill overlooking the town. But to suggest that the colony was created at the same time its walls were built seems a little rash, and any tangible evidence that might support this theory is sadly lacking. Not to mention the fact that coins bearing the inscription *Col Nem (Colonia Nemausus)* were struck in the town well before the reign of Augustus. In fact, these coins have

Nîmes: The statue of Augustus

Nîmes: The Tour Magne

been found in a number of *oppida*, such as **Nages**, throughout the Languedoc region, embedded in deep archeological levels dating from the pre-Augustinian era, proving that Nîmes was a *colonia* well before the advent of Augustus. The third hypothesis is based on the eastern origins, both Greek and Egyptian, of the town of Nîmes. As demonstrated by, for example, the inscriptions covering the mysterious **Temple de Diane** – Diana's Temple – and the oriental ceremonies performed there, the Hellenic influence on the architecture of the town's monuments is quite pronounced. But the key argument used to defend this hypothesis is the extraordinary decoration on the coins, **the bronze asses**, found in abundance on the site of Nîmes. On one side, there is the profile of Augustus, as well as that of Agrippa; on the other, an open-mouthed crocodile, with clearly visible scales and a heavy collar fastened around its neck, tied by a thick chain to a waving palm tree. The meaning commonly attributed to these symbols is straightforward: on one side, Augustus, the founder; on the other, a rather exotic way of recalling how Nîmes was first settled by a group of Roman legionnaires who had served in Egypt. A more plausible explanation, however, would be that these coins, which were struck on a large scale and circulated throughout the Empire, commemorated the Roman victory of Actium, in Egypt, where Augustus and Agrippa together vanquished Cleopatra. Bearing the emperor's image and easily recognisable symbols, the coins would have been designed to recall Rome's glorious victory over the Egyptian crocodile and would have served as an efficient vehicle of Roman propaganda. But one last ambiguity remains – that of Nîmes' title of *colonia*. Was Nîmes really a Roman colony, bearing the most sought after title in the Empire? Or was its rank that of the far less prestigious Latin colony? Although it is difficult to be certain, it seems that the nature of Nîmes' municipal government corresponded more to that of the Latin colonies than to that of the

Nages Oppidum

In the heart of the Garrigue's sweet-smelling jumble of scrubland vegetation, at the top of the steep path that climbs Castels Hill, Nages Oppidum boasts so rich a concentration of ancient remains that it is a truly exceptional archeological site. Dating from the first millennium B.C., Nages Oppidum is typical of the settlements to be found in this area, built on relatively inaccessible rocky ridges and further fortified by solid ramparts of regular stones. Even though partly destroyed now, the colossal towers that once protected the settlement are still sturdy and forbidding, and still tell a very eloquent tale, although some of the finer details may have been forgotten, of times of terrible fear, long vigils, and great battles. Things take on a more human perspective as the path, following the slope, runs next to a series of houses, laid out in geometrical blocks, and separated by parallel streets. Although the design of the whole is well thought-out, living conditions in the single-room houses, equipped with a central hearth, must have been rather uncomfortable. Displays in the archeological museum provide the proof that the inhabitants of this oppidum were farmers and stockbreeders, weavers and potters, soldiers and artists.

Nages Oppidum

Roman colonies, which adhered to the very rigid example set by Rome. Furthermore, the fact that it was governed by a *quattuorviri*, rather than a *duoviri* assembly, which was more characteristic of a Roman colony, indicates that Nîmes was, indeed, a Latin colony. In the light of the city's exemplary growth, however, perhaps its status is of little importance. Indeed, spreading over more than two hundred hectares, and acquiring all the monuments typical of a Gallo-Roman town of the greatest importance, by the 2nd century, Nîmes, with a population of over 20,000, had become the rich capital of a prosperous region.

Nîmes' architectural wealth bears further witness to the city's importance in ancient times. The most famous, and best preserved, of its monuments is the temple known as the **Maison Carrée** – the Square House – which has survived practically intact, its original architectural purity unsullied by later additions or alterations. Built at the end of the 1st century B.C. under the Emperor Augustus, it is the work of an *architectus* from Narbonensis who, despite his provincial Gallic origins, took his inspiration from buildings in Rome. Its simple design is typical of a Roman temple: a flight of fifteen regular steps leads up to the *podium*, surrounded by a colonnade with Corinthian capitals, and to the *cella*, the room dedicated to the god or gods worshipped there, in this case, the Emperor Augustus' two grandsons. Crowned by a leafy scrolled frieze and a cornice with fine decorative brackets, the proportions of this temple attain a degree of perfection, elegance and harmony that are rarely equaled.

The **Amphitheatre**, commonly known as the Arènes, was built in the late 1st, or early 2nd century. Although of a fairly modest size for a building of its kind, it could hold more than 23,000 spectators. Around its oval-shaped arena, the terraces of the *cavea* rise in regular tiers, supported by the two arcaded levels of its exterior wall. Ease of access to and from the terraces was evidently one of the archi-

Nîmes: The Arènes - An interior gallery

tects' major preoccupations. The *cavea* was divided into three *mænia*, each containing ten tiers, and separated from each other by corridors connected by *vomitoria* to the four monumental entrances. Roman society was ruled along such strict hierarchical lines that it was vitally important that access to and use of the terraces, all organised according to the rank and social status of the spectators, should be achieved without conflict, confusion, or any undesirable mingling. Thus carefully segregated, the crowds, buzzing with excitement, could settle to enjoy the violent and bloody gladiator fights taking place below them, cheering and booing their heroes of the day.

Nîmes' fresh water supply, brought by aqueduct from Uzès via the Pont du Gard, was distributed throughout the town from the ancient water reservoir, the ***castellum divisiorum***, by means of an ingenious system of sluice gates and canals.

As the first of the barbarian tribes swept into Provence, Nîmes was unable to resist invasion. And the Visigoths, powerful, belligerent, and little inclined to embrace the Catholic faith which recognised Christ as fully divine, forced the population of Nîmes to adopt their own, Arianistic, beliefs.

The 11th century **cathedral of Notre-Dame-et-Saint-Castor** features a very ancient Romanesque frieze where a multitude of characters busily carved into the stone bring the prodigious story of the Bible to life. The area around the cathedral, known as Old Nîmes, still boasts some fine Renaissance houses with, in Rue de Bernis, mullioned windows, and, in Rue de la Madeleine, facades decorated with sculptured friezes. At number 8, Rue de l'Aspic, three Paleo-Christian sarcophagi have been set into the wall of the entrance porch.

Nîmes' **Archeological Museum**, housed in what was once a Jesuit college, contains collections of protohistoric, Gallo-Greek and Gallo-Roman objects, with pride of place given to displays of glassware, ceramics, coins, bronzes, jewelry and arms.

Nîmes: The castellum

Nîmes:

1 The frieze on Notre-Dame-et-Saint-Castor Cathedral

2 A Paleo-Christian sarcophagus in Rue de l'Aspic

3 Archeological Museum: *Apollo*

4 Archeological Museum: Mosaic

The Pont du Gard

As the Roman Empire expanded into Provence, it soon encountered one of the major problems of the Mediterranean climate – the nearly annual summer drought. This, together with the increasing demands for water associated with rapid urban development, raised the crucial question of providing the new centres of population with adequate supplies. As part of the solution, the town of Nîmes was to be supplied by spring water from Eure, near Uzès, some thirty kilometres away. The supply canal, built of stone, was to have a constant and regular slope, and all obstacles were to be overcome: mountains pierced by tunnels; valleys spanned by aqueducts. As part of this project, the Pont du Gard was built, carrying the canal on its topmost arches, in a single prodigious leap, across the Gardon Valley. The bridge, both colossally delicate and solidly ethereal, was built of great drystone blocks, arranged in three superposed rows of arches, and supported by heavy piers driven deep into the river bed. The blocks were raised using great winches and pulleys, worked by heavy wooden drums turned by the swift, but despairingly static, tread of the labourers who were shut inside for hours on end. The complicated calculations of volume and mass involved in hoisting the enormous blocks to heights of more than fifty metres is a testimony to the exceptional engineering and architectural skills possessed by this nation of master builders.

The stones that protrude from the pillars were used as scaffolding supports. Each arch was built over a wooden frame, laid between two piers on a well-packed pile of sandbags. When the arch was finished, the sandbags were emptied, allowing the scaffolding to be removed.

Why did the Romans perform such outstanding feats of civil engineering? Simply to ensure the continued comfort of the city dwellers, already used to the convenience of fountains and baths equipped with running water!

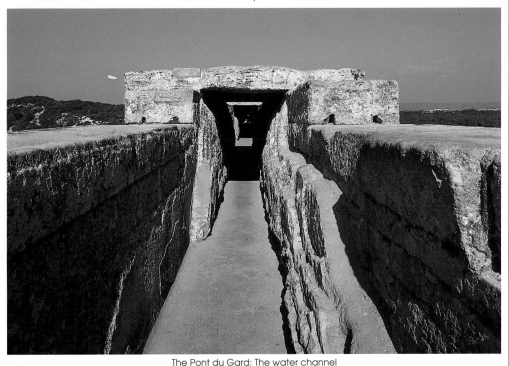

The Pont du Gard: The water channel

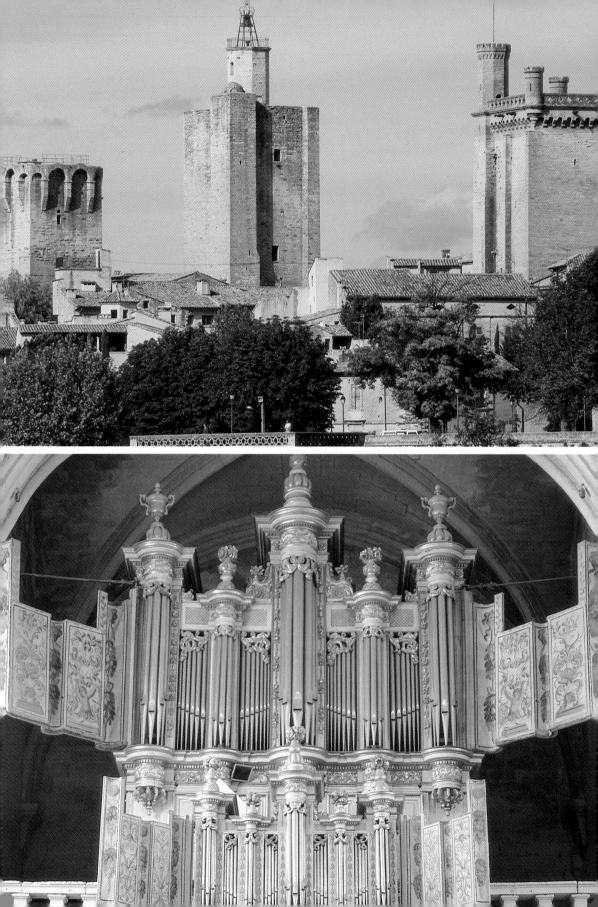

Uzès

Cutting through the soft limestone of the Garrigues, the sides of the Alzon Valley rise suddenly, in places, in white-faced cliffs. Uzès was built on one such steep site, overlooking the river. In the Middle Ages, Uzès was a fortified town, surrounded by ramparts. Later, however, as the manufacture of hard-wearing fabrics in the town's increasing number of drapers' workshops brought prosperity and urban growth, Uzès, becoming uncomfortably crowded, spread outside the confines of its walls, acquiring a number of fine buildings.

The venerable age of the dynasty of the Lords of Uzès, which can be traced as far as the Emperor Charlemagne himself, earned them great distinction among Provence's nobility. Under their rule, Uzès enjoyed an uneventful history, prospering and growing rich, until the Reformation suddenly shattered its tranquillity, splitting the town into two camps, each driven by a faith more fervent than the other, and stirring up intellectual turmoil, with its inevitable consequence: violent, blind fanaticism. Sadly, the gulf that separated Catholic and Protestant then has never really been bridged since. Strangely, it was during this same period, in 1565, that the French Crown bestowed the enviable title of Dukes of Uzès on the town's noble Lords.

The feudal castle of the Dukes of Uzès, appropriately named the **Duché**, or Ducal Palace, is a disparate collection of buildings of various architectural styles, pieced together over the long years of its history. Square and solid, **Bermonde Tower** is an 11th century keep, although its coffered staircase, with its stones cut into diamond-shaped points, shows clear signs of the Renaissance. The **Tour de la Vicomté**, or Viscounty Tower, was added in the 14th century. The façade of the central building was designed by one of the greatest architects of the French Renaissance, Philibert Delorme. Much influenced by Greco-Latin architecture, he set the classical orders of ancient sculpture one above the other in three superposed rows: first the oldest, Doric, order, then regular Ionic spirals, and finally, the leafy profusion of the Corinthian order. The palace's interior and furniture have retained all their ancient splendour, but the Gothic chapel was extensively restored in the 19th century.

Saint Théodorit's Cathedral was built in the 17th century, on the ruins of an earlier cathedral, destroyed during the Wars of Religion. It boasts a magnificent organ, also from the 17th century, which features unusual hinged shutters, used to cover this instrument of pleasure during the solemn period of Lent.

All that remains of the 12th century Romanesque church is the long, tapering, lacy stone spindle of the **Fenestrelle Tower**. Built on a square foundation, it rises to a tiny conical roof in a stack of six successively smaller round tiers. A Romanesque building of great beauty, the repetitive shape of the tower's gemelled bays gives a unity to the whole, while each stage bears a different decoration.

Uzès: The Fenestrelle Tower

Near Saint Stephen's Church (Saint-Etienne), the colossal 18th century **Tour de l'Evêque**, or Bishop's Tower, also known as the Tour de l'Horloge, or Clock Tower, topped with a round turret, still stands guard.

Some of the houses in this area still have their original doors, finely chiseled into convergent beams and diamond points, such as the **Louis XIII door**, in Rue Saint-Etienne. This street leads into **Place aux Herbes**, which is surrounded by perfectly restored covered arcades. The regularly colonnaded 18th century **Hôtel du Baron de Castille** has a well-preserved classical facade.

Just a few kilometres from Uzès, the **Château du Baron de Castille**, restored in the 18th century, is decorated in a similar style. Its long drive, bordered with yew trees, opens onto a row of columns, set in an arc, and crowned with openwork balustrades.

Not far from Uzès is **Eure Spring**, whose waters were once channeled to the town of Nîmes via the Pont de Gard aqueduct.

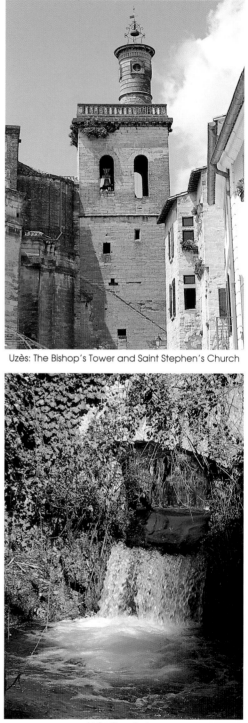

Uzès: The Bishop's Tower and Saint Stephen's Church

Uzès: The Louis XIII door in Rue Saint-Etienne

Uzès: Eure Spring

The Garrigues and The Gardon Gorges

To the south of the Massif Central, the limestone ridges of the Garrigues country of Nîmes rise up towards the mountainous edges of the Cévennes. In ancient times, these infertile heights were sparsely-wooded Mediterranean forest lands, covered in the dark foliage of solidly squat evergreen holm oak, and gracefully airy Aleppo pine. But long years of overgrazing and the ravages caused as fire swept regularly through the unprotected forest gradually destroyed this fragile habitat. Little by little, trees yielded to shrubs and bushes, and the sparse forest gave way to a more resistant form of vegetation – the garrigues, or scrublands – better able to withstand the harsh combination of scorching heat and prolonged drought. With their roots plunged deep into the rocky soil in search of the least trace of water, and their leaves rolled into fine thorns or covered in a waxy film to afford some protection in this hostile, burning environment, each plant in the garrigues competes with its neighbours to exude the headiest, most intoxicating of fragrances.

Lying on the edge of the Cévennes, the castle at **Castelnau-Valence** experienced the worst of the early 18th century Protestant Camisard rebellion. Enthusiastically restored in the 19th century, however, this mighty stronghold has lost none of its original magnificence.

Carved out of the soft limestone into a true canyon, **Gardon Gorges** form a deep furrow surrounded by vertical cliff faces. At the end of a narrow loop in the river, the Pont Saint-Nicolas-de-Campagnac spans the Gardon's clear waters. This elegant bridge, with perfect arches and an openwork parapet, was built by the companions of the Frères Pontifes, a brotherhood of bridge builders who, in the 13th century, under the guidance of Bénézet, builder of the famous Pont d'Avignon, undertook a vast programme of construction work.

Castelnau-Valence Castle

3

THE VAUCLUSE

BETWEEN RHONE AND VENTOUX

FROM THE NESQUE TO THE DURANCE

1

THE AVIGNON REGION

Avignon

In the complicated tangle of watery branches formed where the Rhone is joined by its powerful tributaries, the Ouvèze and the Durance, the slightest hill or the smallest rock rising above the wet plains and grassy banks became the jealously contested object of many bitter disputes. The foaming torrent flowing past the foot of Doms Rock almost certainly gave the Celtic settlement built there its name. *Aouennio* – meaning master of the waters – lived under the protection of its enterprising neighbours from *Massalia*, the Phocaeans, until the Romans, developing their newly conquered territories, made it a self-governing *civitas* of the rich Narbonensis Province.

But the price of so enviable a site – naturally protected and commanding a crossroads position – was bound to be exacted, and, almost inevitably, the town fell prey to the various barbarian tribes that flooded the region, drawn by the brightness of these southern lands. Sieges, battles and raids followed one another in swift succession, each taking its toll, until the last traces of the prosperous days of the *Pax Romana* finally disappeared and Avignon fell into decline, unable to resist the deadly waves of disease and invasion that swept over it.

In the 13th century, caught up in the complex twists and turns of the political fortunes of the Kings of France and the Counts of Provence and of Toulouse, Avignon, proud of its independence and of its status of commune, was to pay dearly for its alliance with the Raymonds of Saint-Gilles, who opposed the Kings of France in the Albigensian Crusade.

Then at last, a clever piece of matchmaking by Queen Blanche of Castille – who married her son Charles, already Count of Anjou, to the

"Sur le Pont ..."

Who can think of the city of Avignon without immediately recalling their first French lessons and that familiar melody, with its ill-pronounced words: "Sur le pont d'Avignon... On y danse, on y danse..."? And its true! They did dance on the bridge! Certainly, some danced "comme ceci", while others danced "comme ça". But little matter how they did it, the important thing is that they danced! Although – and at the risk of shattering a few long-cherished illusions – it seems that they didn't dance on the bridge so much as under it, on the little island, Barthelasse Isle, over which the bridge was built. In the 12th century, a certain young shepherd, Saint Bénézet, received divine instructions (angels, it seems, have a decidedly soft spot for shepherd girls and boys!) to build a bridge over the swift waters of the great river. How could anyone doubt the boy's word as, in one easy movement, he lifted a rock that sixty strong, fully-grown arms would have been unable to budge? Fired with enthusiasm and religious zeal, and supplied with considerable quantities of gold crowns, Bénézet's bridge-building disciples, the Frères Pontifes, set about building their wooden bridge. Set on old Roman piers, its twenty-two arches spanned nine hundred metres across the raging river, over the central island, towards the Philippe le Bel Tower at Villeneuve-lès-Avignon. The Rhone, however, was not about to be beaten, and repeatedly and persistently swept away the bridge's piers and deck until man, tired of rebuilding, was at last forced to admit defeat.

heiress of the Count of Provence – heralded a new period of prosperity for the city of Avignon. But the event which was, more than any other, to earn the city its greatest glory, bringing it fame, fortune and splendour, and promoting it suddenly to the ranks of the great medieval capitals, was the arrival of the papacy in Avignon. With the return of the papal see to Rome, in the late 14th century, Avignon once more assumed its role of provincial town. Although decimated as the plague epidemic of 1720 spread unstoppably from Marseilles, Avignon's population rallied quickly and, when it became part of France in 1791, the city had already recovered much of its former power.

Marking out a vast rounded area, Avignon's **ramparts** were built in the 14th century. Their gates, curtain walls and watchtowers, all carefully guarded, were designed to protect the city from the violent bands of mercenaries that roamed Provence and from the unpredictable rages of its fast-flowing river.

Spanning the river next to a small well-fortified castle, is **Pont Saint-Bénézet**, Saint Benedictus' Bridge – the famous Pont d'Avignon. At one time the bridge boasted twenty-two piers, but over the years the energetic waters of the Rhone have persistently and repeatedly swept away large parts of its bold structure until today, only four arches remain. For many years, the fragile, half-Romanesque, half-Gothic Saint Nicholas' Chapel, on the second pillar, housed Saint Benedictus' relics.

Rising above the Pont d'Avignon are the low, steep cliffs of **Doms Rock**, whose well-laid out gardens offer one of Avignon's most delightful walks. Past mossy hollows and softly babbling fountains, with the heavy foliage of centuries-old trees rustling overhead, neat pathways crunch underfoot, leading to a vantage point that affords the most wonderful view over the Rhone and the town below. And who could resist pausing for just a moment in front of that strange sundial, to see time marked out by the dark line of their own fleeting shadow?

Avignon: The Pont Saint-Bénézet and Saint Nicholas' Chapel

①

②

But the real jewel in Avignon's crown is, undoubtedly, the Papal Palace. An unassailable fortress, the palace is surrounded by blind walls, fortified gates and crenellated keeps, and crowned with bold battlements pierced by narrow, cross-shaped loopholes. Safe behind their curtain walls, and strikingly different in style and decor, are the **Palais-Vieux**, or Old Palace, a sober reflection of the severe character of its founder, the ruthless inquisitor, Jacques Fournier, who later became Pope Bénedict XII, and the much lighter and airier **Palais-Neuf**, or New Palace, designed and built by that lover of art and literature, Pope Clement VI. The portraits of the seven popes of Avignon that hang in the **Salle du Consistoire**, the Consistory, put faces to the anonymous succession of their numbered Christian names, and recall the altogether human side of the papacy. As the seat of the papal courts, this council chamber was the setting for much of the dramatic intrigue of Avignon's eventful history. Its western wall is decorated with frescoes by Simone Martini. Opening off the Consistory, the **Chapelle Saint-Jean**, Saint John's Chapel, contains frescoes by Matteo Giovannetti, painted between 1346 and 1348. These charming scenes demonstrate the artist's new awareness of perspective, giving depth and relief to his work. With its paneled ceiling curved gently into the shape of a ship's keel, the **Grand Tinel** was one of the palace's most impressive rooms. Used as a banqueting hall and reception room, its vast dimensions provided plenty of space for entertaining the popes' many prestigious guests and their large retinues. Before the fire of 1413, the ceiling was stretched with midnight blue cloth and studded with golden stars. Behind the huge fireplace set against the northern wall is **Clement VI's Kitchen**, an unusual room with a pyramid-shaped hood and an immense conical fireplace rising over the hearth. Opening off the Grand Tinel is **Saint Martial's Chapel**, also decorated by Giovannetti. The brightly coloured frescoes covering its walls and vaulted

The Popes of Avignon

By the beginning of the 14th century, dark intrigue, discord and division in Rome led the papacy to seek a quieter climate in which to pursue their pastoral ministry. Far from the turmoil of Saint Peter's city, the Comtat Venaissin, which had become church property in 1274, seemed the perfect spot. And so began the reign of the seven popes of Avignon – all of them French – which lasted from 1309 to 1376. The first of the seven, Clement V, who had taken the decision to leave Rome, established his court in Groseau Monastery, at the foot of Mont Ventoux. The Papal Palace and its collected splendours were the work of John XXII and Benedict XII. In 1348, Pierre Roger, who was to become Pope Clement VI, bought Avignon from Joan I, Queen of Naples and Countess of Provence. But from riches to opulence, from tolerance to licentiousness, and from liturgy to pomp, the Avignon papacy gradually slipped into the grips of the sin of pride. To add to its troubles, all manner of highwaymen, thieves and mercenaries were drawn irresistibly by the city's ostentatious wealth. The solid fortifications that already protected the Papal Palace were no longer sufficient, and, in order to provide Avignon's merchants, artists, pilgrims, monks and nuns with some degree of protection, it became necessary to surround the entire city with defensive walls. As Avignon continued to live in such extravagant luxury, even its greatest advocates began to lose faith in it and the great Italian scholar and poet, Petrarch, who lived there, condemned it as "the sewer of the universe". It was time to return to Rome. But, for more than thirty years, the return was to be delayed as pope and antipope engaged in the futile quarrels of the Great Western Schism.

ceiling demonstrate the virtuosity of these Italian painters, the forerunners of the Renaissance masters. It was here that the cardinals of the Sacred College would meet to elect their pope. The **Chambre de Parement**, or robing room, antechamber to the pope's audience room, contains three Gobelins tapestries. The **Chambre du Pape**, the vast papal bedchamber, lies at the heart of the palace. Against a sky-blue background, its walls are painted with elegant leafy scrolls, twined together into a complex interlacing pattern, where quarrelsome birds and cheeky squirrels frolic gaily, while birds, imprisoned in gilded cages painted on the window frames, seem poised to sing the lament of their lost freedom. The *Studium*, Benedict XII's private study, has a beautiful terracotta tiled floor. One of the palace's finest rooms is the **Chambre du Cerf**, or Stag Room, Clement VI's private study, whose remarkable decor – fishing and hunting scenes populated by deer, ferrets and falcons – is really rather on the secular side! The elegant and soberly decorated **Clementine Chapel**, built in pure Gothic style, opens through a large bay window onto a loggia overlooking the palace's main courtyard. It was from this window, known as the **Fenêtre de l'Indulgence**, now perhaps rather over-enthusiastically restored, that the popes dispensed their blessing on the faithful crowds gathered below. The ribbed vault of the immense **Salle de la Grande Audience**, the Great Audience Chamber, rests on five ribbed pillars. A fresco by Giovannetti, representing the prophets against a sky-blue background studded with golden stars, covers the vault of the eastern bay, where the *Tribunal de la Rota* used to meet. This court is thought to have taken its name – meaning wheel – from the circular bench where the thirteen judges appointed by the pope would sit. Used for some time as an arsenal, the **Salle de la Petite Audience**, or Small Audience Chamber, is decorated in grisaille, or monochrome, frescoes, illustrating the unusual theme of military trophies.

Avignon: The Papal Palace - The floor of Benedict XII's private study

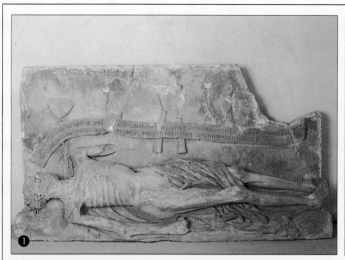

Avignon: The Petit Palais Museum -

① Cardinal Jean de Lagrange's tomb

② Botticelli: *Madonna and Child*

③ *Madonna and Child*, depicted between two saints and two benefactors (Avignon School)

④ Liberale da Verona's *Abduction of Helen of Troy*

The Petit Palais Museum

When the popes moved to Avignon, the city's bishops took up residence in the Petit Palais – the Little Palace. Later, the palace was converted into a museum devoted to the works of Middle Age and Renaissance artists. The fantastic richness of its decor provides the perfect setting for the subtle transition from the primitive works displayed in the first gallery to the brilliant exuberance of the Italian masters hung in the other galleries. The museum also houses fragments of the tomb of Cardinal Jean de Lagrange – one of Charles VI's ministers – showing a realism and pathos that hint at the early days of baroque art. In the middle of the 19th century, patiently gathering works from all the great Italian cities, the Marquis Compana built up a personal art collection of inestimable value. Financing his passion for the arts through his activities as banker, moneylender, and pawnbroker in Rome, he was convicted of embezzlement, and forced to sell all he owned. It was Napoleon III who, in the name of France, bought the entire Compana collection. Since the Second World War, much of the original collection has been restored to the museum. In the early 14th century, the Florentine School abandoned the unnatural rigidity of Byzantine art for a style that allowed much greater freedom of composition. Taddeo Gaddi's *Madonna and Child* provides a perfect example of this new influence. Next to a small wedding chest by Domenico di Michelino that tells the tale of poor Susanna, is a very beautiful 15th century *Madonna and Child* by a very young Botticelli. Liberale da Verona's *Abduction of Helen of Troy* and, of particular note, Vittore Carpaccio's *Holy Conversation*, from the 16th century, are just two of the many masterpieces displayed in the Petit Palais Museum.

Avignon: The Petit Palais Museum - Vittore Carpaccio's *Holy Conversation*

AVIGNON SOUVENIRS

1

2

Just opposite the Papal Palace, the **Hôtel des Monnaies**, or Mint, was built in the 17th century as the residence of the papal legate, Cardinal Borghese. The dragons and eagles of the Borghese family coat of arms rear up proudly on the garlands of fruit and flowers that stream from the mouths of four grimacing monsters.

Avignon's heart beats to the rhythm of Place de l'Horloge, where the Jacquemart Tower, rising above the **Hôtel de Ville** (Town Hall), is all that remains of the Gothic convent of the Dames-de-Saint-Laurent.

The number of churches, chapels and convents (complete with bells) that sprang up on Avignon's every street corner in the 14th century, under papal rule, was such that the writer Rabelais dubbed it *the ringing city*.

Notre-Dame-des-Doms Cathedral, with its square bell tower, has undergone considerable changes over its long lifetime. Originally Romanesque, and already embellished in the 12th century, the arrival of the popes in the 14th century heralded the cathedral's finest hour, as side chapels, a chancel and a monumental apse were added to its single nave. The 17th century, with its distinctly baroque leanings, left the Romanesque nave perhaps just a little over-decorated, with the poignant and slightly affected figures of Saint Martha and Mary Magdalene emerging from inextricable jumbles of garlands and interlacing patterns of foliage. Flanked by griffins, the white marble bishop's throne is still draped in rich purple cloth, and the tombs of Popes John XXII and Benedict XII, rising in fine, intricately lacy stonework above their respective recumbent figures, are anything but humble.

Saint Peter's Church owes the magnificence of its facade, with its almost excessive decor of scrolls and tongues of fire, to Flamboyant Gothic architecture. The two wooden panels of its doorway are sculptured in the same style. Carved in solid walnut by Antoine Volard for a fee of just sixty crowns, they are, today, of inestimable value. On the left panel, the Archangel Michael can be seen striking the devil,

Notre-Dame-des-Doms: Detail of the bishop's throne

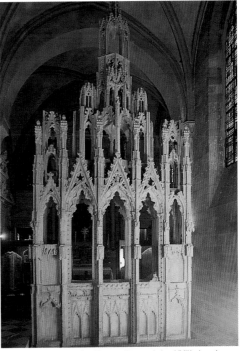

Notre-Dame-des-Doms: Pope John XXII's tomb

while Saint Jerome pursues his journey in the company of his faithful friend, the lion. On the right, the Archangel Gabriel, with the fine features of a girl's face and finger raised, announces the coming birth of Jesus to Mary, seated on a large chair. The door's central pier is decorated with a *Madonna and Child*.

The altar front in **Saint Didier's Church** depicts the moving scene of the *Bearing of the Cross*, with Mary swooning with the agony of seeing her son taken away to be crucified.

It is just not possible to mention every church by name, but **Saint Agricol's**, with its Gothic facade and its famous 1525 Doni altarpiece showing Imbert Boachon's unusual interpretation of the *Annunciation*, is worth the detour.

Like its churches, Avignon's Penitent brotherhoods were numbered by the dozen. The walls of the **Chapelle des Pénitents-Noirs** bear a very strange decoration of bubbling clouds, from which the gentle faces of winged cherubs emerge, with a central pair of chubby angels carrying John the Baptist's head on a platter!

Many of Avignon's private mansions also bear the marks of the city's former magnificence. The **Palais du Roure**, Roure Palace, with its Gothic facade of interlacing spiny branches, is a particularly fine example.

In the 18th century, Avignon's printed cotton fabric industry was concentrated in **Rue des Teinturiers**, where the waters of the Sorgue provided both a source of energy and a convenient means of rinsing the dyed materials. At one time, six workshops provided employment for more than five hundred people here, and today, a number of paddle wheels, some of which still turn, can still be seen.

In 1039, the nuns of Notre-Dame-des-Doms founded **Saint Ruf's Abbey** outside the city's ramparts, near a Paleo-Christian necropolis. Today, only the transept, the bell tower and the church's chancel remain. Carefully decorated, it must once have been an elegant building, although subsequent modifications have marred the architectural harmony and beauty that it might once have possessed.

Avignon: Saint Peter's Church - The left door panel

Avignon: Saint Ruf's Abbey

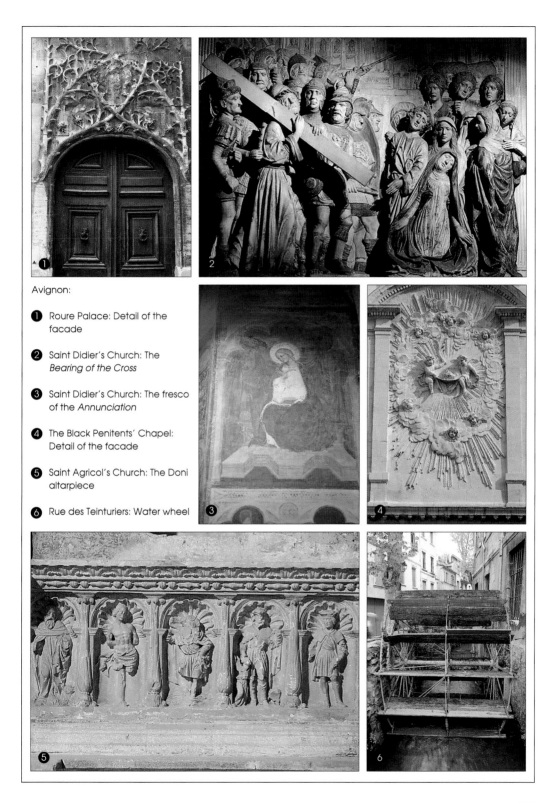

Avignon:

1. Roure Palace: Detail of the facade

2. Saint Didier's Church: The *Bearing of the Cross*

3. Saint Didier's Church: The fresco of the *Annunciation*

4. The Black Penitents' Chapel: Detail of the facade

5. Saint Agricol's Church: The Doni altarpiece

6. Rue des Teinturiers: Water wheel

1 The Lapidary Museum: Bas-relief from Cabrières-d'Aigues

2 The Lapidary Museum: Relief work carved at the top of a decree made by Demosthenes

3 The Lapidary Museum: The *Noves Tarasque Monster*

4 The Vouland Museum: Glazed earthenware from Marseilles

5 The Requien Museum: Detail of the herbarium

Museums in Avignon

The **Lapidary Museum**, located in the former Jesuit chapel, houses some of Provence's most remarkable ancient artifacts. Among an exceptional collection of antique statues depicting a wide variety of themes, the *Noves Tarasque Monster* closes its claws over the heads of two bearded old men, throwing back its head in laughter. From the maiden coiling her hair about her head and *Bacchus* from Saint-Gabriel, to the *Pourrières Venus* and the faithful portraits of Rome's emperors, the pieces displayed here come from sites all over Provence. Even without its head, the colossal statue of *Jupiter*, discovered at Séguret, is a fine work. Dressed in the imperator's fringed tunic, he is shown leaning on a wheel and an eagle – the two symbols traditionally associated with him. One of the most fascinating pieces is the bas-relief, found at Cabrières-d'Aigues, representing a riverside towing scene.

Avignon's natural history museum, the **Requien Museum**, founded in the 19th century by the botanist Esprit Requien, houses fine geological and paleontological collections. But the museum's best piece, reflecting Requien's own particular interest in fauna and, more especially, flora, is his magnificent herbarium.

The **Louis Vouland Museum** contains faience (glazed earthenware) from the workshops of Marseilles, Montpellier and Moustiers.

The **Calvet Museum**, created in the 18th century by a professor at Avignon's faculty of medicine, Esprit Calvet, as a "public place of cultural interest", has become, through gifts and purchases, a fine museum. Unfortunately, it is temporarily closed to the public.

In **Villeneuve-lès-Avignon**, the museum boasts a 15th century altarpiece, *The Crowning of the Virgin Mary*, by Enguerrand Quarton, discovered in the last century by Mérimée.

The Villeneuve-lès-Avignon Municipal Museum: *The Crowning of the Virgin Mary* by Enguerrand Quarton

①

②

Villeneuve-lès-Avignon

Built right on the river's edge, Villeneuve-lès-Avignon owes much of its fame and fortune to its position on the historical frontier between crown lands and papal property. Closely guarded by the Philip the Fair Tower, the famous Pont Saint-Bénézet provided the tenuous link between this new town (*ville neuve*) near (*lès*) Avignon and the old city.

In search of houses and lands in keeping with their rank, it was not long before members of the papal court crossed the bridge to settle in the *livrées* of the new town. At the same time, a number of religious establishments, such as the Val-de-Bénédiction Chartreuse, sprang up. When the General of the Carthusian Order conveniently stood down after being elected as pope, Cardinal Etienne Aubert became Pope Innocent VI. Mindful of the debt he owed the Carthusians, the new pope gave his *livrée* at Villeneuve-lès-Avignon to be used as their monastery. Extensive embellishment works began with the pope even lending his favourite painter, Matteo Giovannetti, to decorate the papal chapel with fine frescoes. Always very fond of this Charterhouse, it was Innocent VI's express wish that he should be buried here. His finely ribbed stone mausoleum can be seen in the church. Gradually, the Val-de-Bénédiction Chartreuse became the largest Charterhouse in France. It had three cloisters: the Little Cloisters, hidden deep within the maze of monastic buildings; the Graveyard Cloisters, where a row of cells, opening onto tiny private courtyards, were once occupied by the Fathers; and the largest of the three, Saint John's Cloisters, where the fountain is protected by a rotunda.

Today, the great gates of Saint Andrew's Fort, with their twin round towers, guard only the ruins of Saint Andrew's Benedictine Abbey and the 12th century Notre-Dame-de-Belvézet Chapel. And what remains of the streets and walls of the town itself has long since been abandoned to wild grasses and birdsong.

Villeneuve-lès-Avignon: Innocent VI's mausoleum

The Val-de-Bénédiction Chartreuse - The Little Cloisters

Villeneuve-lès-Avignon: Frescoes in the chapel

1 Barbentane: The castle

2 Barbentane: The Anglica Tower

3 Notre-Dame-de-Grâce: A votive offering

4 Caderousse: Saint Michael's Church

5 Roquemaure: The castle

Between Avignon and Orange

Dating from the 17th century, **Barbentane** Castle was built along the very strict architectural lines of the classical style, deemed to be the very height of elegance and harmony. The perfect symmetry of its facade, ordered in neat rows of bay windows, is further emphasised by the formal ponds and flower beds of its vast grounds. An old 14th century keep, the Anglica Tower, overlooks the town.

The interior walls of **Notre-Dame-de-Grâce**, near Rochefort-du-Gard, are covered with votive offerings, poignant reminders of the fervour and constancy with which the faithful are wont to implore the holy mother of Jesus.

Once a forbidding keep, the castle at **Roquemaure** lifts its still proud remains towards the sky. In 1314, Clement V, the first of the Avignon popes, came here to die. For many years, this little town on the banks of the Rhone was a stopping place for the heavy boats that passed to and fro, laden with cargoes of wine from the Châteauneuf and Tavel vineyards. On the opposite bank, the valley is guarded by Leris *Castellum*, now **Hers Castle**.

Today, all that remains of the *château neuf*, the new castle, built by the popes at the height of their glorious reign over Avignon, are a few ruins. And, paradoxically, it is their palace in Avignon, the Palais-Vieux, that bears the name "old". It may lie in ruins, but the popes' country residence, having given its name to one of the most famous Rhone valley wines – Châteauneuf-du-Pape – is far from forgotten.

Some historians affirm that it was just a few kilometres upstream, at **Caderousse**, that Hannibal and his army – complete with thirty-seven elephants – crossed the Rhone in the year 218 B.C.. The village, often flooded in the past, and still constantly wary of the river, is now protected by a dyke. The Romanesque church of Saint Michael's contains an elegant chapel, built in the Flamboyant Gothic style by the local lords, the De Grammont family.

The Popes' Wine

Around the popes' new country residence – their *château neuf*, or *new castle* – terraces of light, warm, alluvial soil climb the slopes from the riverbank. By a wonderfully fortuitous, but discreet, process of heat exchange, the soil absorbs the warmth of the sun by day, stores it up, and releases it again at night, when frost may bite and kill. Ever since vines were first planted here in the 14th century, the red and white wines they produce have enjoyed an excellent reputation. Today, the strictly regulated Châteauneuf-du-Pape *Appellation d'Origine Contrôlée* is a guarantee of both origin and quality. The Winegrowers' Museum, housed in the perfect setting of Father Anselme's Cellar, gives an insight into the age-old art of cultivating the noble vine. It also boasts a vast cask, dating from the Middle Ages, which would once have contained the very same glowing wine that filled the sparkling glasses on the tables of the Papal Palace.

Father Anselme's Cellar: 14th century wine cask

2

FROM ORANGE TO VENTOUX

Orange

The site of *Arausio*, which later became Orange, was one of the traditional stopping places along the ancient trade routes. Set in rolling lands where the Aigues (whose name, appropriately, comes from the Provençal word for water) meets the Rhone, the advantages of settling in such a site were many. And, so it was that, long ago, the obscure Celtic tribe of the *Tricastini* stopped here and settled down. Later, waves of tribes from northern and eastern Europe swept down through the Rhone valley, drawn to this land of golden sunlight. From 120 B.C. onwards, the Cimbri and Teutones invaded the region, posing a serious threat to transalpine Gaul, which had hitherto been the preserve of Rome's expansionist ambitions. Responding to this new danger, the Roman army, under Servilius Cæpio, drew within sight of the *Tricastini* settlement, charged with the particularly difficult and dangerous task of stopping the intimidatingly aggressive and courageous Teutonic giants dead in their determined tracks, whatever the cost. But, poorly led, the army was thrown into confusion, harried, and finally routed, suffering so humiliating a defeat that word of it soon made its way back to Rome, and to the ears of the ambitious Consul Marius. Seizing the occasion as an ideal opportunity for furthering his career, Marius, in the year 102, advanced to meet the Nordic tribes in battle and defeated them soundly near the as yet insignificant hamlet of *Aquæ Sextiæ*, which would one day become Aix-en-Provence. Several decades later, veterans of the second *Gallica* legion came to settle in *Arausio*, making it a Roman colony, ranked by Pliny the Elder in his *Naturalis Historia* among the greatest towns of the Roman province of Narbonensis. As part of Rome's colonisation policy, veteran legionnaires, at the end of their period of military service, were given lands in the new Roman territories. The records of these land transactions were kept in perfect order, and often revised, and indeed, the museum in Orange still has a number of fragments of engraved marble, bearing the carefully recorded details of the cadastral land survey. There are, in fact, three separate registers, showing analyses by plot and by type of land, covering vast areas from Châteaurenard to Orange, and from Orange to Montélimar. According to these documents, it seems that the town of Bollène was located at the intersection of the two major routes that ran through the land in Roman times, the *cardo* and the *decumanus*. In particular, the registers recorded the legal status of the land, classifying each plot according to whether it was considered as Roman land, colonial territory, an indigenous tribute-paying estate, or state-owned property.

But Orange's real claim to fame is its pair of Roman monuments, from the 1st century B.C. – its Théâtre Antique (Roman Theatre) and its Arc de Triomphe (Triumphal Arch).

Orange's **Roman Theatre** is one of the best-preserved of the entire Roman world. Rising in semicircular arcs, the terraces of its *cavea* are supported by the hillside, while, at its foot, its semicircular shape is echoed by its *orchestra*. Facing the terraces is a vast rectangular building, the *scæna*, which served both as stage decor and wings. Decorated with statues and columns, the stage wall could accommodate scenery backdrops and all the complicated machinery needed to stage ascensions, disappearances and other special effects with the maximum of dramatic impact. The already remarkable quality of the theatre's carefully designed acoustics was further enhanced by a roof, which covered the stage and acted like a huge megaphone. The groove into which it fitted can still be seen. To protect them from the sun, a canvas roof, or *velum*, was stretched over the spectators and attached to masts by ropes. An imposing statue of the Emperor Augustus, sculpted on a scale to match that of the theatre itself, has been restored and placed in the stage wall's central niche – a fitting homage to the man who gave Orange its theatre.

The **Triumphal Arch** opens onto the ancient Roman road, the *Via Agrippa*, which ran from Arles to Lyon. Set firmly on three arches, it was built to commemorate the heroic deeds of the Second Legion, in the north of Narbonensis Province. The two upper levels are decorated with trophies of coats of arms and a complete collection of tackle from the ships that served in the Roman wars. The confused detail of the battle frieze shows the triumphant legionnaires, and the poignant image of their prisoners, chained, hopeless and dejected.

Orange: The Triumphal Arch - *Trophies*

Orange: The Triumphal Arch - *Naval designs*

Orange: The Triumphal Arch

Orange: The Roman Theatre - The stage wall ▶

Between Aigues and Lauzon

During the Middle Ages, heavily fortified walls were built around **Camaret-sur-Aigues**. Parts of these walls, and notably the famous Porte de l'Horloge, or Clock Gate, with its twin round towers and charming bell tower, have survived virtually intact.

The castle at **Mornas**, which was owned by the Bishops of Arles, was taken and rebuilt by the Count of Toulouse in 1197. During the Wars of Religion, it was besieged by the Protestants who threw the hapless inhabitants, all faithful Catholics, off the top of the cliff.

Formerly the property of the Popes of Avignon, the town of **Bollène** occupies a privileged site on the river terrace formed by the rapid waters of the Lez. Safe within its protective ramparts, the town, with its rich residences and great churches, is full of old-world charm. The former collegiate church of Saint Martin's has been restored a number of times

Camaret-sur-Aigues: The Clock Gate

Jean-Henri Fabre's House

Reputed for his ill temper and his sometimes rather extraordinary ideas, the learned botanist and entomologist, Jean-Henri Fabre, was, at the end of the 19th century, the subject of much public debate. Moving from his native Rouergue region to live in Avignon, but unwelcome among the leisured and educated classes of the town, he began to seek a place better suited to the pursuit of his work. In 1879, he found a *harmas* near Sérignan, whose lands had been left untended for so long that they had become a paradise for all the creeping, crawling, flying and swarming creatures of Provence. In this living entomological laboratory, as he called it, Fabre dedicated his life to the study of this tiny animal kingdom, leaving his collections and other works – including his famous research on the strange processionary pine caterpillar and the region's fungi – to posterity.

Jean-Henri Fabre's House: The main room

Jean-Henri Fabre's House: Insects

since it was first consecrated in the 12th century. More a sturdy keep than a delicate belfry, its bell tower rises above the nave, flanked with heavy buttresses. Situated at the highest point of the town, it commands a wonderful view which takes in the long finger of fertile land, bordered by the outstretched line of the Donzère-Mondragon Canal as it separates from the Rhone, doubling its course.

Suze-la-Rousse Fortress was built at the top of a hill, among the soft green foliage of an ancient oak forest. Solidly built and set squarely on its colossal earth embankment, it is surrounded by machicolations and crowned with battlements. Built in the 14th century, at a time when siege was giving way to open conflict waged on the fields of battle, it is one of the latest examples of a structure built as a (theoretically, at least) impregnable fortress. The Renaissance, however, was to have a rather mellowing influence on the fortress' harsh character. Inside, frescoes tell the tale of the Siege of Montélimar, just one of the terrible episodes of the Wars of Religion, during which the Lord of Suze-la-Rousse, seriously injured, is said to have urged his poor mare, also on her last legs, to carry him home "to die at Suze" with him.

Right next to **Visan**, the chapel of Notre-Dame-des-Vignes, Our Lady of the Vines, dedicated to the Holy Mother, boasts a fine statue of the Virgin Mary, framed in a gilded wooden panel dating from the 13th century.

The commandery of the Order of the Knights Templars at **Richerenches** provides convincing proof that these soldier-monks were past masters in the defense of the highways and byways traveled by medieval pilgrims.

Built against the cliff, the church at **Montségur-sur-Lauzon** is, to all appearances, an unremarkable building, with a virtually blind facade and a tiny bell tower. Its outer simplicity, however, conceals the fact that, inside, a cave extends into the very depths of the rock.

Just a few kilometres to the north, **Chamaret** belfry can be glimpsed.

Suze-la-Rousse: The castle

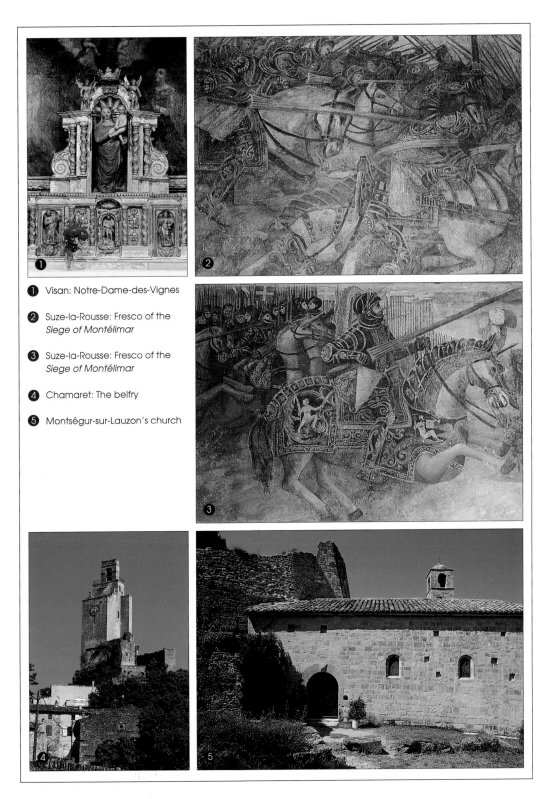

1 Visan: Notre-Dame-des-Vignes

2 Suze-la-Rousse: Fresco of the *Siege of Montélimar*

3 Suze-la-Rousse: Fresco of the *Siege of Montélimar*

4 Chamaret: The belfry

5 Montségur-sur-Lauzon's church

Grignan

Grignan Castle was once owned by François de Castellane d'Adhémar de Monteil, Count of Grignan, Lieutenant General of Provence from 1669 to 1714, and son-in-law of Madame de Sévigné, who never really forgave him for stealing her daughter from her. A *castrum* existed on the site as early as the 11th century. In the 13th century, a fortress was built, and in the 15th, it was transformed into a residential manor. In the 16th century, Louis Adhémar, Governor of Provence, rebuilt the facade and courtyard, giving the castle an odd sort of architectural unity, despite the clear Renaissance flavour of its southern facade, a Gothic wing and Classical apartments. The furnishings in the castle's maze of rooms, including an Italian cabinet and Aubusson tapestries, reflect a little of the high society brilliance of Grignan's heyday. In Saint Saviour's Church, Madame de Sévigné's tomb is identified by a plaque.

Grignan: The castle - An Aubusson tapestry

Madame de Sévigné

On November 2nd, 1679, Madame de Sévigné closed a long letter to her daughter with the words, "Farewell, my dear child – I love you beyond that which it is possible to love", so resuming the overwhelming intensity of a mother's love and affection for her daughter, married to the Count of Grignan, Lieutenant General of Provence. Lighthearted and witty when recounting the spicier pieces of gossip concerning life at the royal court, she became solemn and serious when sharing her more philosophical or moral thoughts. A highly accomplished storyteller, with a gift for keeping her reader in suspense, her beautifully composed letters, written in a flowing and natural style, were to become, after her death, a masterpiece of French literature. During her frequent visits to her daughter, she would often go to think and reflect in the cool of Rochecourbière Cave.

Rochecourbière Cave

CY GIT
MARIE DE RABUTIN CHANTAL
MARQUISE DE SÉVIGNÉ
DÉCÉDÉE LE 18ᵉ AVRIL 1696.

Grignan: Madame de Sévigné's tomb

❶

❷

The Coronne Valley

In the 14th century, the northern border of the Comtat Venaissin – the papal domain that stretched across the Vaucluse Plain – underwent a number of changes. Continually preoccupied with extending the lands under their direct rule, the popes set their sights on the tiny, but rich, valley of the Coronne, with its prize, the town of **Valréas**. For a certain financial consideration, the Dauphin Humbert I, Count of Viennois, ceded his rights over Valréas to Pope John XXII. Acquiring first Visan, then Grillon, the popes pursued their expansionist policy until the French monarchy, under Charles VII, decided to put a stop to this subtle annexation of their kingdom. Without actually being forced to return any lands already bought, the popes were denied the right to make any further purchases in the region. The papal enclave of Valréas was born and, even after several centuries of centralisation under the Re-

public, has remained a little Vauclusian wart on the face of the *département* of the Drôme. Dating from the 11th and 12th centuries, Notre-Dame-de-Nazareth Church in Valréas has a fine Romanesque portal. Its three doors open below trefoil arches, and the central panel is crowned by three regular rows of finely sculptured semicircular archivolts. The 18th century Simiane Castle was once the home of Pauline de Grignan, known affectionately by her grandmother, Madame de Sévigné, as her "pretty child". Today, it houses Valréas' town hall.

Just a few leagues away, the little medieval town of **Taulignan** still has its merry-go-round of watchtowers and curtain walls and its ancient streets still boast a number of Renaissance facades with light accolade arches over their doorways, and fine mullioned windows.

At the foot of the first slopes of the Baronnies, the village of **Venterol**, set hard against its protective mountainside, gazes out over the rich plain of the Comtat Venaissin.

Valréas: Detail of the church's portal

Venterol

Nyons

Surrounded by a high ridge of mountains, the town of Nyons nestles at the mouth of the narrow gorges carved out by the Eygues (the Aigues). Ever since the 14th century, the single arch of a Romanesque bridge has spanned the clear waters of the river here, opening up a passageway to Orange and Montélimar. Randonne Tower, built in the 13th century, lifts the elegant and elaborately airy crown of its bell tower against a backdrop of deep blue sky, while, in fitting contrast, sunlight filtering through a series of little openings barely illuminates the dark paths of the long gallery of Rue des Grands Forts, cut right into the rock. With an exceptionally mild climate, Nyons has become the centre of Provence's olive growing country, and its oil mills still turn here to this day. But, more than just the capital of the olive, Nyons also offers the discerning palate the chance to savour truffles, honey and apricots.

Smooth and Golden

In Nyons, the olive groves bear the names of forests, and the view of the Nyons basin from the top of the Vaux Mountains cannot fail to call to mind the landscapes of Greece. Nyons' little wrinkled black olives are harvested very late, in December, or even in January. Crushed, squeezed, and pressed cold, the olives give a smooth, rich, and sweetly perfumed oil, of such high quality that it bears that prestigious mark of excellence, the *Appellation d'Origine Contrôlée* of Nyons. Appropriately, Nyons has a musuem dedicated to the olive, where the traditional tools and skills used to cultivate the trees and produce the oil are presented. But this ancient art can only be fully appreciated by visiting to one of the old oil mills, where the screw of the press turns constantly above the millstone's wide jaws.

Nyons: Randonne Tower

An oil mill press

❶

❷

Vaison-la-Romaine

Well before the arrival of the Romans, the Vocontii, a people of Celtic origin, settled between the Rhone and Mont Ventoux, in this land where the Eygues (the Aigues) and the Ouvèze – their translucent green waters speckled with foam – cut across the complex relief of the Baronnies. Instead of attempting to tackle the impassable barrier of the Dentelles de Montmirail, the Ouvèze, much more reasonably, skirts around the northern side of their rocky heights. Here, in the trough of a wide curve in the river, the large fortified village of *Vasio Vocontiorum*, capital of the Vocontii, harboured a flourishing market and a number of shrines dedicated to local gods.

Ever hungry for new lands to conquer, the Roman Empire spread into the territory of the Vocontii and decided, with or without their consent, to turn it into a *civitas* – a Roman city-state, consisting of the *urbs*, or town (the state's religious, economic and political centre) and the rural area under its protective rule.

The territory of the southern Vocontii tribes, the *Civitas Vasiensium*, under its alliance with Rome, became a federated Roman city. Under Augustus, the *Pax Romana* (the Roman Peace) demanded complete submission to the imperial Roman power but, in return, brought Vaison a guarantee of prosperity and local influence highly valued by the noble classes and the local elite. Vaison earned its fortune through trade and, paradoxically, it was by its river, the Ouvèze, that it grew rich, becoming a port for the barge-rafts on animal skin floats that navigated its turbulent waters. In exchange for its grain and wine, Vaison imported the luxury goods that were to contribute to the Romanisation of its native population. By the 1st century A.D., Vaison had become a fully-fledged Gallo-Roman town. By accepting to settle within the confines of the Roman town, and by modeling Vaison's urban plan on that of the mighty Roman capital, the Gallic elite began a process of Roman integration that was to allow them access to all civil and religious honours and, eventually, to the prestigious status associated with Roman citizenship.

Naturally, Vaison began to acquire all the fixtures and fittings that accompany a well thought-out urbanisation process. The first priority in this Mediterranean climate plagued by drought was, of course, water. Attempts to master the supply and use of this life-giving liquid resulted in some remarkable feats of civil engineering. Vaison's aqueduct, stretching ten kilometres from Groseau Spring, at the foot of Mont Ventoux, to the town itself, drops by two hundred metres. And Vaison's fountains and the baths – equipped with a clever hypocauste underground heating system that graduated the temperature in the different rooms from cold, through warm, to hot – consumed such quantities of running water that a sophisticated system of drains, relying on natural gravitation, had to be built to empty the used water into the river below the town.

The need to span the rapid waters of the Ouvèze with the least difficulty made the narrowest part of the river, where it slips between steep rocky banks, the natural choice for the site of a bridge. With its single arch opening wide over the waters, Vaison's Roman bridge has resisted all the onslaughts of time and has withstood all the furious rages of its powerful river, whose violent and destructive mood swings, once witnessed, are never forgotten.

The town fans out from its two traditional main routes, the *cardo* and the *decumanus*, onto its Roman roads and their adjacent streets, with their perfectly preserved pavement. Archeological excavations, covering an area of about fifteen hectares, have unearthed the remains of a number of *domus*, large private houses characterised by exceptional comfort, luxury and beauty. Three of these colonnaded palaces – the House of the Messii, the House of the Silver Bust, and the Dolphin House – open onto fresh gardens where babbling water drops in gentle cascades from basin to basin, among a decor of fine mosaics. The richness of the colours and the astonishing skill with which the shape and relief of the Peacock Villa's pavement are rendered, make it a work of exceptional artistry. Although Vaison must once have boasted the public buildings, such as an amphitheatre, found in any Gallo-Roman town, the only remains discovered to date are those of a theatre, built against Puymin Hill. Statues of Diadumenos, Hadrian and Sabina would once have adorned the niches of the galleries of Pompey's Portico. In addition to its Roman heritage, Vaison-la-Romaine is rich in medieval history. The cathedral of Notre-Dame-de-Nazareth, built on the very pagan foundations of a former Roman temple, is a fine example of Provençal Romanesque architecture. Its cloisters, with their enigmatic inscription and strange double-faced cross, together with Saint Quenin's Chapel, with its triangular apse, add the finishing touches to the historical portrait of this centuries-old town.

The Théo Desplans Archeological Museum

Vaison-la-Romaine's Archeological Museum lies almost hidden in a basement in the Puymin Quarter, although it houses most of the major finds unearthed during the digs undertaken at the beginning of the century. The exhibition rooms are arranged around a central, glazed *atrium*. One is dedicated to a collection of epigraphic objects, mainly funerary and religious inscriptions. Another houses the finest of Vaison's treasures – its statues. The nudity of Hadrian's statue is in striking contrast to the heavy folds of his wife Sabina's dress. And, while Claudius harangues the crowd, Domitian sports a chiseled breastplate. But did this head, wreathed in laurel leaves, once belong to Apollo or Venus? Finally, there is the museum's pride and joy, a silver bust of one of the town's notables, discovered in 1926 in the Villasse Quarter.

Vaison: Saint Quenin's Chapel - The chevet

Saint Quenin's Chapel: Merovingian stonework

The silver bust of one of Vaison's notables

The Dentelles de Montmirail

Immense convulsions of the earth's crust once forced thick layers of Jurassic limestone upwards into a bristling monster's spine of sharp needles. Then, with skillful fingers, Mother Nature worked the exquisitely fragile forms of this long rocky ridge – so aptly named the Dentelles de Montmirail, after the French word for lace, *dentelle* – and set it against a background of deep azure blue. Below, the hillside takes on a more gentle form, covered in a light gauze of golden broom and dotted with the dark green of pine and leafy oak.

The village of **Crestet** lies in the shadow of its huge 12th century castle, which looks out distrustfully through the openings that pierce its forbidding facade, while narrow streets, lined with old houses, climb right up to the fortress. Well protected by a natural amphitheatre of white rock, **Séguret** revels in the peace and tranquillity that has always suffused this privi-

Crestet: A narrow street

Séguret: The church

leged site. With old narrow streets struggling up and tumbling down its slopes, a belfry, a fountain and a 12th century church, the village has lost none of its former charm. And its vineyards, climbing to the foot of the cliffs, are heavy with the ripening promises of fruity Gigondas wine and heady well-being.

The village of **Le Barroux** is dominated by the massive bulk of its castle. Built in the 12th century by the Lords of Les Baux, this heavy, impregnable white stone building was designed exclusively for defensive purposes. Then, beginning in the 16th century, successive generations of the Lords of Le Barroux set about transforming this protective shell of a fortress into a fine Renaissance residence, where no detail – from large mullioned windows, to delicate galleries opening onto an Italian loggia – was to be neglected.

Between Le Barroux and the quaintly-named village of **Suzette**, crowning a hill surrounded by vineyards, the road sinks into the folds of rock that lie at the foot of Mont Saint-Armand.

The journey down to **Malaucène**, at the heart of a sparsely-wooded and sweet-smelling forest, is one of pure delight. A stop at Groseau Spring, whose abundant cool waters rise at the foot of the cliff, is not to be missed.

Nearby, the naively simple chapel of **Notre-Dame-du-Groseau**, with its square floor plan and tiny bell tower, is all that remains of an ancient monastery, said to date back to the dark centuries of the Merovingian era. Restored to its former glory in the 11th century by the Benedictine monks of Saint Victor's in Marseilles, the monastery was chosen by Clement V, who was pope from 1305 to 1314, as a place of retreat, far from the worries and summer heat waves of his capital, Avignon.

The rocky barrier of Montmirail, which rises to the relatively modest altitude of only eight hundred metres, certainly cannot claim to be a mountain range. Nevertheless, set in the heart of a typically southern landscape, its vertical rock faces and spiky ridges undeniably lend it something of an Alpine air.

Suzette and the Dentelles de Montmirail

Mont Ventoux

In the heart of a rolling landscape of gentle alluvial valleys, a single mountain, a lonely peak, rises above the plain. Although Mont Ventoux, at an altitude of 1,912 metres, cannot compare with its far loftier neighbours, the Alps, it boasts all the features typical of any mountainous area. Built in the late 19th century, the road from Saint-Estève to Le Chalet-Reynard starts its difficult ascent through a luxuriant cloak of vegetation. With each step, the flora changes from sparsely-wooded forest, drowsy with the heady perfume distilled by the heat of the sun, to the beech and fir trees of higher grounds and colder climates, with every possible combination covering the slopes in between. Emerging at last from the trees, and dazzled by the sudden intensity of sunlight, the road continues up the last hellish inclines frequented by the Tour de France cycling championship. A roadside memorial commemorates the death, due to overexertion, of Tom Simpson during the 1967 race. At this altitude, the rock, shattered and reduced to shingle by the grinding jaws of frost, is so pure and white that only the snow that accumulates in heavy compact layers from the very beginning of winter is whiter still. The view from the summit, which is crowned by a radio relay and meteorological and radar stations, takes in the level plane of the sea, shrouded in a light haze and lost in the infinite blue of the distant horizon, the rolling contours of the Alpilles and Mont Sainte-Victoire, the soft green ribbon cut by the Rhone, the agglomeration of Marseilles, and, almost within arm's reach at the foot of the mountain, the village of Bédoin, clustered around its Jesuit style church. But the name of Mont Ventoux (*vent* means wind) is synonymous with wind. Never gentle breezes, the winds here vary from strong northerly to biting gale, with the master wind, the mistral, bringing bitterly cold weather, and driving cloudy masses in its stormy paths.

Mont Ventoux: The summit

3

FROM THE NESQUE VALLEY TO APT

The Vaucluse Plateau

Set between, and running parallel with, the Ventoux and Lubéron ranges, is the wide, rolling anticline of the Vaucluse Plateau. Although no mountain range, these hills, at an average altitude of 800 metres, form a barrier to be reckoned with, and any river determined to set its course here must, like the **Nesque**, carve its way through in deep gorges, following the natural faults in the plateau's rocky mass. This vast limestone table bears all the features typical of any karstic relief: flat-bottomed dolines carpeted in red earth, chasms oozing with wetness as water seeps through porous rock, and tortuous caves, part of the subterranean hydrographic network whose waters rise to the surface, in places, as resurgent springs. Perfectly adapted to this arid, stony soil, the garrigue scrublands are interspersed with strips of forest. And soft billows of lavender fields, shimmering in the hot wind, roll away to a distant mauve horizon.

In the single nave of the priory church at **Saint-Christol**, the capitals of the columns in the apse sprout prickly acanthus leaves, while, at the base of their shafts, nasty little gnomes contort their ugly faces in jeering laughter.

At **Méthamis**, a section of the plague wall, built in 1720 to try to contain the epidemic, has been rescued from ruin, and restored.

In May, processions of pilgrim farmers come to Saint Gens' Hermitage, near the village of **Le Beaucet**, to ask their patron saint, Gentius, to spare them the summer's drought.

Saint-Christol: The priory church - *A gnome*

The Nesque Gorges

Méthamis: The plague wall - A guardroom

Venasque:

1 Notre-Dame Church: The door of the tabernacle

Pernes-les-Fontaines:

2 The Covered Cross

3 The Cormorant Fountain

4 The Ferrande Tower

5 The Ferrande Tower: Fresco of *Saint Christopher*

6 The Ferrande Tower: Fresco depicting knights at battle

Venasque and Pernes-les-Fontaines

It may have given its name to the Comtat Ve-naissin, but that is certainly not **Venasque**'s only claim to fame. Guarding the ancient road across the Vaucluse Plateau, the village is set firmly on a steep-sided rocky needle. When the slope becomes too sheer, Venasque simply turns its streets into stairways, and continues its climb to the very edge of the ravine, and Notre-Dame Church. Since it was first conse-crated in the 12th century, this church has been extensively rebuilt. On its gilded taber-nacle, Christ breaks bread with his disciples in Emmaus. Next to the church is Venasque's an-cient and mysterious baptistry. Laid out in the simple form of a Greek cross, with the capitals in its northern apse decorated with primitive sculptures, it is one of Provence's oldest relig-ious buildings, although much of its rare archi-tectural wealth was spoilt by unfortunate resto-ration work in the 12th and 19th centuries.

By a happy coincidence, the ancient settle-ment of *Paternae*, now the town of **Pernes-les-Fontaines**, grew up on a site where the phreatic table simply overflowed with water. Today, the waters that gave the town its name pour forth in gently babbling pearls of light from more than thirty elegant fountains. The handsome bird on the Cormorant Fountain, built in 1761, harmonises well with the per-fectly worked decor of Notre-Dame Gate. To cross the stone bridge between the two stout corbelled towers, and to pass the chapel of Notre-Dame-des-Grâces, is to be carried back through time to the days and nights when alarm bells would ring out to warn against the many dangers – mercenaries, plague and Hu-guenots alike – that so often assailed the town. Such prudence has preserved the fine frescoes in the Ferrande Tower. Painted between 1280 and 1290, they present a mixture of styles, where portraits of the Virgin Mary and Saint Christopher alternate with scenes from the life of Charles of Anjou, brother of Saint Louis.

Venasque: Notre-Dame Church - The baptistry

Pernes-les-Fontaines: Notre-Dame Bridge and the keep

①

②

Carpentras and its Vicinity

Bordered to the north by the chiseled lace of the Dentelles de Montmirail, **Carpentras** lies in the centre of a delightful natural basin. The heavier clouds seem to avoid it, and the mistral, broken by the sharp ridges to the north, doesn't recover its mighty breath until well beyond the town. Founded on a small knoll by tribes of Celtic traders, Carpentras is still a busy centre of commerce. In the Middle Ages, the town became the capital of the Comtat Venaissin, and was visited by popes and cardinals alike, coming in search of a little peace and quiet far from the worries of Avignon. Until the Revolution, Carpentras had a large Jewish ghetto. It still has one of the oldest synagogues in France, and the southern doorway of Saint Siffrein's Cathedral, decorated in the Flamboyant Gothic style, is still known as the Porte Juive, or Jews' Gate. Near the ruins of the old Romanesque cathedral, which still lifts the mutilated arcades of its dome skywards, are the remains of an ancient Triumphal Arch. Built in the 1st century A.D. in honour of the Emperor Augustus, it commemorates his victory over the Gauls, who, nevertheless, put up quite a fight before submitting to the heavy yoke of Roman imperial rule. Two prisoners, their hands tied behind their backs, can be seen reflecting sadly upon their unenviable fate. Largely destroyed by fire in 1713, all that remains of the Medieval town hall is the bell tower, its twisted wrought iron heart boldly silhouetted against the sky.

Not far from Carpentras, the cemetery at **Mazan** has more than sixty Gallo-Roman sarcophagi. At **Sarrians**, the church's dome, resting on squinches and dating from the 11th century, provides a fine example of early Romanesque architecture. Near **Beaumes-de-Venise**, the chapel of Notre-Dame-d'Aubune boasts a square Romanesque bell tower, pierced with single bays decorated with streams of leaves and grimacing monsters.

Mazan: Gallo-Roman sarcophagi

Carpentras: The bell tower

Sarrians: The church's 11th century dome on squinches

L'Isle-sur-la-Sorgue

Cradled in the arms of the Sorgue – which lend the town something of a Venetian air – L'Isle-sur-la-Sorgue has always known how to take full advantage of its watery site, and the mossy paddle wheels dotted along the races full of dark rushing water once powered mills, presses, fulling machines and pestles. The Classical facade of the 17th century former collegiate church, Notre-Dame-des-Anges, belies the rich decor of its baroque heart with, in particular, a great gilded wooden glory, where graceful angels flutter around a crowned Virgin Mary.

Not far from there, at **Le Thor**, the quiet waters of the Sorgue reflect an idyllic landscape, a bridge with short arches, and the untroubled outline of the church of Notre-Dame-du-Lac. Its rigorous design, based on the regular and pyramidal construction of its octagonal bell tower, makes this church one of Provence's finest examples of Romanesque architecture.

Thouzon Cave

Three kilometres to the north of the village of Le Thor, Thouzon Cave was discovered in 1902 in what was once a quarry. At the foot of a limestone massif of the Cretaceous period, the cave was formed by the particularly energetic erosive efforts of an underground river. Seeping rainwater has hung the ceiling with abundant sprays of slender, golden, tube-like rocks, whose close-packed little columns shoot a dense forests of needles down towards the cave floor. The light, playing on the many different shades of calcite, bathes the cave in the warmest tones. Glowing red draperies and small natural limestone weirs, called *gours*, overflowing with ochre milkiness, are just some of the many works of art left behind by the waters that once surged, streamed and dripped here.

Thouzon Cave

Fontaine-de-Vaucluse

Apart from giving its name to the town of Fontaine-de-Vaucluse, the spring *(fontaine)* at Vaucluse is so typical an example of a resurgent underground river, that its name is cited as the universal reference for this hydrological feature. Rising from the unfathomable depths of a chasm at the foot of the cliff, its waters roar over tumbling rocks in a bubbling cascade. The Romans worshipped this capricious deity, until, in the 6th century, Saint Veranus felt called to tackle the difficult task of transforming their pagan practice into the rather more Christian one of adoring the Virgin Mary. Built in the 11th century on the site of a very old priory, records of which go back as far as the 10th century, Saint Véran's Church houses the saint's tomb and relics. Legend tells how, empowered by divine grace, he rid the region of that strange and evil monster, half dragon, half serpent – the ferocious Coulobre.

"The Sound of that Sweet Spring..."

As witnessed by the little canal that runs the length of the river's race, the Romans were the first to spot Vaucluse Spring's *vallis clausa*, or closed valley, and to harness its waters. But it was Petrarch, Italian poet and friend of the Avignon popes, who, upon discovering the spring, came here to sing of his passionate, but chaste, love for the beautiful Laura of Noves. From the moment he first set eyes on her beloved face, one fateful day in April 1327, until his death, he bore for her the fierce devotion that was to inspire his *Canzoniere*, a moving love song of three hundred and sixty seven poems. Fleeing the dreadful memory of the plague epidemic that struck Avignon in 1348 and took his beloved from him, he ended his days in Italy, where he was never quite to forget "the sound of that sweet spring".

Fontaine-de-Vaucluse: A Gallo-Roman fountain

Fontaine-de-Vaucluse: Petrarch's Column

A miraculous deliverance? Or more simply, perhaps just the allegorical representation of how, before the irresistible advance of Christianity, paganism was to be crushed and killed like a pernicious beast. The church's high wall is surrounded by a cornice decorated with modillon brackets, where the sculptor has carved the faces of men and the heads of various animals, some as exotic as the lion, others as common as the bat and the fox. Sculptures of an ox and a wolf commemorate the miracle performed by the hermit Gentius who lived near Le Beaucet and who delivered the village from another dreadful pest – a terrible she-wolf. By some great divine mercy, Saint Gentius captured her, subdued her, and, as a sign of her new harmlessness and complete submission, even yoked her together with an ox. The castle, set into the cliff face, was built to guard this place of pilgrimage.

At the bottom of the town, Petrarch's Column stands as a silent reminder of the poet's love for his lady, Laura.

Fontaine-de-Vaucluse: View of the castle

Fontaine-de-Vaucluse: Saint Véran's Church - The modillon brackets

Mills and Caves

It was in the 15th century that the clear and plentiful waters of the Sorgue were first harnessed to turn the busily chattering wheels of paper mills, first grinding, then pressing, and finally, mixing the different raw materials – cotton, linen and hemp – into the thick pulp that was to become paper. Since 1981, Vallis Clausa Mill has rediscovered the joys of the skills of the paper makers of old, and, following the same methods used in the 15th century, produces "hand made" paper, whose thick and noble leaves are encrusted with grasses and petals, or traced with the perfect calligraphy of the illuminator's voluptuous hand.

Speleologists, geologists and explorers alike couldn't fail to be drawn to a resurgent source as exceptional as Vaucluse Spring. Tribute is paid to one of their illustrious number, Norbert Casteret, in the strange and wonderful decor of his *Monde Souterrain*, his Underground World.

During his long career as a speleologist, Casteret explored more that two thousand caves and chasms. It was he who dared to follow, and hence make known, the complicated passageways that lead to the heart of the Pierre-Saint-Martin Chasm. Fascinated by the mystery surrounding the true source of the Garonne, and determined to elucidate it, he traced the river to the Maladeta Mountains. During his different expeditions, Casteret collected a vast number of samples, and here, in this place dedicated to the delights and techniques of speleology, nearly four hundred limestone rock formations from his collection are displayed in the superbly reconstituted decors of their original, and often quite inaccessible, sites. There is an interesting presentation of how, from hypothesis, through investigation, to final results, the mystery of the source of the Sorgue was solved.

Vallis Clausa Mill: Beating the cloth into pulp

Vallis Clausa Mill: Drying the paper

Vallis Clausa Mill: Mixing the paper pulp

N. Casteret's Underground World: Cave paintings

Gordes

Set against an intensely blue sky, the houses of the little town of Gordes flow gently over the hillside, as the pure Provençal light, catching their facades, brings out their warm ochre tones. Crowning the hill is the squat form of Saint Firmin's Church, with its tiny wrought iron bell tower. The castle, which once belonged to the Agoult-Simiane family, was rebuilt during the Renaissance. Taking the simple form of an elongated quadrilateral, it is flanked, to the north, by a pair of large round towers, while its southern facade sports watchtowers and mullioned windows. Inside, a magnificent fireplace, encompassing a pair of doors set one either side, boasts an exuberant decoration of elaborate pilasters and flowering garlands. The staircase, which is a brilliant example of stereotomy – that fine art of cutting stone, wood, or other noble construction materials – leads to the Vasarely Museum.

Vasarely

When Victor Vasarely settled in France in 1930, he had already established a solid reputation. Having studied the very innovative architectural principles of Bauhaus in Budapest, he was destined for a career as a graphic artist. In his work, the line – that most basic of all geometric forms – repeated in orthographic projection, and colour, defined in strong, bright tones, are combined, arranged, and gradually, almost imperceptibly, distorted until the whole picture takes on depth and volume as the rigorously flat surface of the canvas seems to stretch into three dimensions. And the wonder of the optical illusion doesn't stop there as, with every movement of the eye, shapes are reversed, directions are turned around and volumes blur into one. A master of geometric abstraction, Vasarely is one of the most representative figures of the virtual kinetic art movement. Surviving all the whims of fleeting fashion and standing the test of time, his works remain marvels of simplicity and pure gaiety.

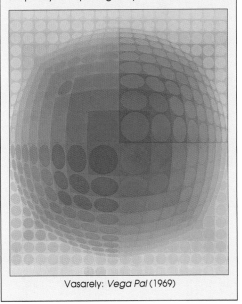

Vasarely: *Vega Pal* (1969)

Gordes: The castle - The staircase

Not far from Gordes, the stone dwellings of a mysterious ancient hamlet, the **Borie Village**, raise their inscrutable facades and a thousand and one questions which, as yet, remain largely unanswered. Stone is in abundant supply here, and, roughly hewn into thick slabs, called *lauzes*, it is used to form frames, walls and roofs alike. Laid one by one, using the ancient technique of dry-stone construction, the *lauzes* gradually arch inwards to form a gently vaulted roof, crowned with one last slab. But whether shepherds' huts, barns, or permanent farm dwellings – the mystery remains. In spite of the presence of a communal bread oven, the absence of a cemetery and a place of worship makes it improbable that this was ever a village settlement as such.

Saint-Pantaléon lies clustered around its 12th century Romanesque chapel. Successively rebuilt and added to, the original 5th century building has been somewhat altered by time's passage. Cut directly into the stone, a series of sarcophagi form a rocky necropolis.

Saint-Pantaléon: The chapel and the necropolis

The Lavender Museum

On the road from Gordes to Coustellet, set among the billowing lavender fields of the estates of the Château du Bois, the Musée de la Lavande, the Lavender Museum, opened in 1991, provides the key to fully understanding and best appreciating how this elegant and precious plant is cultivated and used. Acclimatised long ago to the hot summers of the Vaucluse Plateau, the lavender bushes spread out in rolling waves that lap gently at the museum's very doorstep. The lavender – from both the age-old wild lavender bushes and the richer, more resistant natural hybrid *lavendin* – is harvested in summer. The museum houses a collection of very old, fat-cheeked copper stills where, in days gone by, the slender blue-tinted stalks would yield up their precious aromatic oil, lavender oil, which is not only traditionally considered to be the very essence of perfect cleanliness, but is also said to possess an impressive range of therapeutic properties.

The Lavender Museum: A still

Sénanque Abbey

If perfection belongs to the realm of the supernatural, then there is something undeniably divine about Sénanque Abbey. But that the abbey should have been founded by monks of the austere Cistercian rule is perhaps not surprising, because the very essence of Sénanque's beauty lies in its unadorned grandeur, in the isolation and silence, the peace and serenity espoused by these monks from Cîteaux. It was in 1148, in the narrow, lonely valley of the Sénancole – throbbing with heat and the strident discord of cicadas, its sheer sides covered in the garrigue's scrubland vegetation – that monks from Mazan in Vivarais began building the abbey. A supreme homage to harmony and light, perfectly in keeping with the architectural principles of the Cistercian community, the abbey, with its regular blond stone walls and its slightly rough pearl grey roof, catches the sunlight and plays with the shadows. The church is built to the simplest of plans, with a vast and airy barrel vaulted nave of dazzling whiteness, and a perpendicular transept, forming that unmistakable sign of the Christian faith – a Latin cross. The abbey's perfection of proportion and volume renders any need for further decoration not only superfluous, but undesirable, and, undistracted by statues or scrolls, garlands or stained-glass, spires or pinnacles, the good brothers were free to pursue their lives of quiet soul-searching in close communion with God. The only decoration to be found is in the cloisters, where the capitals are twisted with blossoming palmettes, and a grinning monster, either demon or Tarasque, symbolises temptation and evil. Clustered around the cloisters, are the chapter house, the refectory, the *chauffoir*, which, as the only heated room in the abbey, was where, from matins to vespers, the more educated monks turned their skillful hands to calligraphy, and finally, the lay brothers' buildings, where the monks of more lowly birth laboured and lived.

Sénanque: The cloisters

Sénanque: *The Tarasque Monster*

Roussillon

Roussillon is one of those charmed villages that enjoy both a privileged site and wonderful surroundings. Balanced on a needle of rock, Roussillon's old houses glow with the warm colours so characteristic of the soils on which it is built. In order to better admire the hills of ochre rock that gather all around, the village is perched on the highest point. Its streets rise in long steps that bite into the steep slope, and end in platforms that offer splendid panoramic views. Boldly outlined against the halo of light haze that shrouds Mont Ventoux and the Lubéron, and fringed by dark green oak and pine, are the fire-red cliffs, the Val des Fées (Valley of the Fairies), the Falaises de Sang (Blood Cliffs) and the Chaussée des Géants (Giants' Causeway).

Twenty kilometres to the west, at **Rustrel**, the forces of erosion have quarried the tender rock into the very aptly named Provençal Colorado.

Red and Gold

Only Nature herself would dare attempt so extravagant a decor of red and gold. Ochre is a siliceous rock belonging to the sandstone family. Solid yet soft, compact yet crumbly, it falls easy prey to the sculptural virtuosity of erosion, and is soon transformed into the stone-capped pillars of fairy chimney stacks. And, as if bold shape were not enough, Nature adds the final touch to these, her works of art, by painting them in vivid shades of ochre red. Through its varied composition, and by chemical reaction, the rock, which contains small quantities of iron oxide, yields an unlimited range of colours. Golden white, saffron yellow, blood-red and crimson – the cliffs are radiant as, in the changing light of the Provençal sun, each finely carved rocky face burns with amarathine shades.

Roussillon: The needles in the Val des Fées

Apt and its Vicinity

All that is known for certain about the Roman colony of *Apta Julia* is the location of its theatre, traces of which can be seen in the basement of Apt's museum, among a large collection of antique stonemasonry. In fact, Apt was so often raided and invaded by the barbarians that, when at last they withdrew, they left little more than a few bloodied ruins. Life, however, could be so pleasant in this sheltered valley where cantaloupes, watermelons and cherries already grew in profusion. In the 14th century, the Avignon popes, inclined to forget that gluttony is a deadly sin, were particularly fond of the local specialty – crystallised fruit. Generations later, the people of Apt still master the art of spiriting away a fruit's water to replace it with that simple natural preservative – sugar. This delicacy brought the town fame and fortune, and today, Apt is proud to call itself the worldwide capital of crystallised fruit.

The cathedral's treasure includes a fine embroidered linen cloth, known, quite incorrectly, as Saint Anne's shroud. Restored in 1930 by the famous Gobelins tapestry makers, it was woven at the end of the 11th century in Damietta, in lower Egypt. Thought for many years to be a Saracen standard captured during the First Crusade, it is in fact part of a ceremonial robe. The cathedral's crypts, sunk deep into the foundations, were built to house the relics of Saints Anne, Auspice and Castor, to whom devoted crowds of pilgrims would flock in search of miracles and forgiveness.

Part of the *Via Domitia*, the **Pont Julien** was built in the 1st century B.C.. The bridge, with its three open arches, still spans the waters of the Calavon which, by a strange toponymical trick, changes its name, becoming the Coulon. **Saint-Saturnin-lès-Apt** once bristled with fortifications behind three separate rings of defensive walls. Today, their remains are overshadowed by the ruins of the castle and its fragile Romanesque chapel, Saint Saturnin's.

The Pont Julien

1 Grambois: Notre-Dame-de-Beauvoir Church

2 La Tour-d'Aigues: The castle's portal

3 La Bastide-des-Jourdans: A chapel

4 Ansouis: Saint Martin's Parish Church

THE LUBÉRON AND THE DURANCE

The Lubéron

The long limestone barrier that stretches in a gentle curve between the gates of Cavaillon and Manosque is known, perhaps rather grandly, as the Lubéron Mountains. Split into two unequal parts by the deep and mysterious Lourmarin Fault, the Lubéron does indeed rise in rounded domes to an altitude of 1,125 metres at Mourre Nègre to the east, although, to the west, the Petit Lubéron's pointed and jagged peaks do not even reach heights of 800 metres. But that is not the Luberon's only paradox. The contrast between its north- and south-facing slopes is so striking that its ridge forms a dividing line between two entirely distinct landscapes. While the northern slope is steep and studded with rocky stumps to which its villages cling, the southern slope, under the even foliage of its orchards, leads gently down towards the banks of the Durance.

The villages of the Aigues area – **La Bastide-des-Jourdans**, once confined within curtain walls, not far from its citadel, **Grambois**, whose church, Notre-Dame-de-Beauvoir, houses a 12th century fresco of Saint Christopher, **La Tour-d'Aigues**, overshadowed by the ruins of its Renaissance castle, and **Ansouis**, nestled up against the forbidding walls of its castle, whose portals open in a monumental arch – all lend the gentle southern slopes of the Lubéron a great architectural harmony.

In the 12th century, the heretical *Vaudois*, or Waldenses, arrived in the Lubéron, and an atmosphere heavy with religious fervour and the

Ansouis: The castle

threat of barely contained violence began to develop. In such a climate, the Lords of Oppède soon saw it as no more than their sorry duty to massacre the sect's followers.

In 1970, the discovery of a mausoleum next to an ancient necropolis confirmed the Gallo-Roman origins of the village of **Cucuron**. In the Middle Ages, the villagers took refuge in the *castrum* and reinforced the ramparts. Cucuron's church, Notre-Dame-de-Beaulieu, is remarkable for its tympanum, decorated in a highly original geometric pattern.

From the height of its great castle, **Lourmarin** looks down over its famous combe – the spectacular result of an immense fracture that occured, long ago, deep within the earth's crust. With its spiral staircase, capped with an elegant copula, and its monumental fireplaces, Lourmarin Castle is typical of the gracious residences built during the French Renaissance. The famous French writer, Albert Camus, who so loved the luminescent skies of the Durance Valley, is buried here.

Cucuron and Notre-Dame-de-Beaulieu

Lourmarin: The castle

The Waldenses

Although the true origin of their name is unclear, it seems that, around 1170, a little-known merchant from Lyons, a certain Peter Vaudes, Valdes, or Waldo, founded, directed, or inspired the "poor men of Lyons" to form a new religious group, which, adopting its leader's name, became known as the Vaudois, or Waldenses. The doctrine of these Christians was simple, being based on – and this was the rub – a return to poverty, a knowledge of Scripture obtained by direct reading of the Bible, and preaching. But the Catholic Church, whose religious monopoly had been openly challenged by the Waldenses, was not to tolerate such an attack, especially since Waldensian teaching and administration of the sacraments called into question both the Catholic doctrine of the adoration of the saints and the validity of Mass. Condemned as heretics by the Lateran Council in 1179, the Waldenses dispersed into Italy and Provence. In 1545, tired of having its authority undermined, and as an act of revenge for the sacking of Sénanque Abbey, the Church decided that, with the help of God and the troops of the Baron of Oppède, president of the Parliament of Aix, the Waldensian villages in the Lubéron were to be destroyed. In just five days, these infamous troops swept through more than twenty villages and hamlets, including Mérindol, Lacoste and Lourmarin, razing them to the ground, and even wiping some of them off the map for good. Massacring three thousand Waldenses and capturing six hundred more to serve as galley slaves in the royal fleet, they left the Lubéron reeling under the violent blow it had been dealt – a blow heavy with the impending threat of the fanaticism and intolerance of the bloody Wars of Religion soon to come.

Entangled in the twists and turns of its ramparts, **Buoux Fort** was designed to resist the longest of sieges. Its grain silos, hollowed out of the solid rock, are solemn reminders that adequate provisions were the key to survival. The magnificent village of **Bonnieux**, with its private mansions, such as Rouville House, which today houses the town hall, shares similar origins. Perched on top of an oppidum, the church, with a Romanesque nave and a Gothic apse, provided a focal point for the local population which, as it grew, gradually spilt down the village's slopes. The new church, built at the foot of the hill in the 19th century, houses four 15th century primitive paintings illustrating the classical theme of the Passion.

Completing this impressive series of perched villages are **Lacoste**, with its grand castle, home to the infamous Marquis de Sade, **Ménerbes**, balanced on a sheer-sided rock, and, of particular note, **Oppède-le-Vieux**, with its citadel's imposing ruins and fine 16th century church, Notre-Dame.

Bonnieux

Ménerbes

Bonnieux: The church - *The Flogging* (15th century)

Lacoste

1 Caumont-sur-Durance:
The Chartreuse de Bonpas

2 Caumont-sur-Durance:
Saint Symphorian's Chapel

3 Noves: The church

4 Orgon: The church

Sailing up the Durance

Caumont-sur-Durance, with Saint Symphorian's Chapel, lies on the right bank of the Durance where the **Chartreuse de Bonpas** calmly watches over an ancient thoroughfare. In the days when fording places were few and far between, and often controlled by unscrupulous bandits who happily fleeced any would-be travelers, the Frères Pontifes, that famous order of bridge-building monks, built a solid bridge here so that all good pilgrims should find safe passage, or *bon pas*, across the river. Later, the Knights of Saint John, then Carthusian monks, settled in the nearby monastery.

Home of Petrarch's true love, Laura, **Noves** once commanded one of the rare fords on the Durance. Near the ramparts, Saint Baudile's Church – its chevet decorated with arcatures – was once part of the town's defensive system.

Bristling with battlements and powerful buttresses, the church at **Saint-Andiol**, near Cavaillon, still looks every inch the citadel, as it jealously guards its treasure of 18th century fine gilt wooden paneling.

In earlier times, **Orgon** was surrounded by ramparts, and the old town, with its narrow streets and opulent houses, prospered by the crowds of pilgrims that flocked to Notre-Dame-de-Beauregard, built on the very top of the cliff. Fine as this church may be, however, Orgon's 14th century parish church, Notre-Dame-de-l'Assomption, is every bit its equal.

At the foot of the Lubéron Range, the ancient settlement of the Cavares tribe, *Cabellio*, once clung precariously to the cliff tops of Saint James' Hill (Colline Saint-Jacques). With the advent of the Roman conquest and the return of peace, **Cavaillon** began to spread, finding life more comfortable at the foot of the cliff, on the edges of the plain that was to make its fortune. Taking advantage of its location on the banks of the Durance and on the *Via Domitia*, the town developed into a thriving centre of trade. A fragile Roman arch, decorated in

Saint-Andiol: The church - Wooden paneling

Cavaillon: The Roman arch

delicate leafy patterns and fluttering with birds and butterflies, was restored in the 19th century. Throughout the Middle Ages, Cavaillon was ruled by its temporal and spiritual lord, its bishop. Bearing witness to the town's former religious importance are Saint James' Chapel, perched on the cliff near the cool and shady hermitage, and Saint Véran's Cathedral, with the corners of its pentagonal apse hidden behind fine fluted columns decorated with prickly acanthus leaves. Inspired by their heightened aesthetic sense, the baroque artists of the 16th and 17th centuries decorated the interior of the cathedral in a profusion of detail that borders on the excessive. In the adjoining cloisters, a sundial, bearing the proud and very pagan head of good old Cronus, god of time, prompts poor sinners to prayer, for the last day is nigh! In the 18th century, Cavaillon's large Jewish community built a synagogue which, with a wrought iron balustrade and a particularly beautiful interior, is a masterpiece of architectural harmony and elegance.

The narrow **gorges of the Régalon**, so sheltered and so protected, provided Neolithic man with a safe place of refuge, even if the torrent was prone to swell suddenly in the wake of the Mediterranean's violent storms.

Cadenet is the birthplace of the famous "drummer boy of Arcole", André Estienne, immortalised by the sculptor Amy in his statue, the *Tambour d'Arcole*. Having engaged against the whole of Europe in bitter struggles, the French revolutionaries were to win victory only by acts of outstanding courage. In 1796, at Arcole, the fearless young Estienne swam the Alpone, the Venetian river where the French and Austrians were to do battle, and sounded the battle drums behind enemy lines. Taken by surprise, and believing they were surrounded, the Austrians beat a hasty retreat! The 17th century parish church at **Le Puy-Sainte-Réparade** boasts a baroque altarpiece by Claude Routier, a sculptor from Aix. Near the ruins of the medieval castle is an 11th century chapel dedicated to Saint Réparade.

The Régalon Gorges

Cadenet: The *Tambour d'Arcole*

Silvacane Abbey

Drowsing peacefully on the banks of the Durance, Silvacane Abbey's restful atmosphere belies the dramatic trials and tribulations of its past. In the Middle Ages, the banks of the Durance blurred into marshlands here among a glistening forest of reeds, the *silva canna*. Although not really isolated, the site was particularly insalubrious and inhospitable, and few considered it a fit place to live until, finding it well suited to their chosen ascetic lifestyle of hard work and solitude, a handful of monks from Saint Victor's Abbey in Marseilles settled here. In the 11th century, their decision to affiliate their tiny community to the strict, but flourishing, Cistercian order brought them good fortune and the promise of a bright future, as the Counts and noble Lords of Provence donated lands and other gifts to the abbey. The marshes were improved and the abbey prospered until, in the late 13th century, those all too human failings of greed and envy brought the monks of Silvacane into conflict with the brothers of Montmajour. Their quarrel was so bitter that it seems it even came to blows. Shortly afterwards, the abbey was pillaged by the Lord of Aubignan's men, and finally, the exceptionally bitter winter of 1364 froze the very hearts of the abbey's vines and olive trees. This last blow was too much for Silvacane, and the abbey fell into decline, although, even today, with its church topped with a little decapitated bell tower, Silvacane is still a magnificent sight. Stenciled against the gilded blue Provençal skies, the church's windows and oculus illuminate and give life to the pure forms of the nave's high vaulted ceiling. The cloisters are surrounded by monastic buildings: *the armarium*, or library; the vaulted chapter house; the parlour, the only point of contact with the outside world; the *chauffoir*, the only heated room in the abbey; the less austere, more ornamented refectory; and, upstairs, the monks' dormitory.

Silvacane Abbey: The cloisters

4

PAGNOL'S PROVENCE

THE AIX AREA

AROUND SAINTE-BAUME

MARSEILLES AND ITS COAST

1

AIX AND ITS REGION

Between the Lubéron and Salon

The E.D.F. (Électricité de France) Canal follows what was once, a million years ago, when it flowed directly to the sea, the original course of the Durance. In 1909, the region to the south of the canal was shaken by an earthquake. The church at **Rognes**, although damaged, still boasts a number of fine altarpieces. On either side of its 17th century high altar, its nave is lined with altars dedicated to the saints of Provence. At **Lambesc** (once a principality belonging to King René), the church lost its spire but is still a respectable size.

Nestling in the leafy grounds of **Château-Bas**, the ruins of Vernègues' Roman temple lend their support to Saint Césaire's Chapel.

Rognes: Detail of an altarpiece

La Barben

Former residence of King Réne and, later, the Forbin family, La Barben Castle is surrounded by formal French gardens, designed by Le Nôtre. Constantly improved and embellished, the richness of the castle's decor was matched only by its beauty. The main hall, decorated with Spanish leather from Cordoba, the ceilings, and Pauline Borghese's boudoir, still bear witness to the greatness of its former glory. The good-natured, docile hippopotamus has become the symbol of La Barben Zoo, where as many as two hundred different species of animal can be seen. The castle's old sheepfold now houses a terrarium, an aquarium and an aviary.

La Barben Castle: The kitchen

La Barben Zoo: Rhinoceroses

1

2

Salon-de-Provence

However one looks at it, Salon-de-Provence occupies a truly privileged site. To the north, the Durance Valley leads to the gates of Avignon. To the south, Berre Lagoon opens onto the Mediterranean. Not far to the southwest is the old Provençal capital of Aix-en-Provence. But the best lies to the west, where the wide open spaces of the Crau Plain were to bring the town fame and fortune. The people of Salon soon realised that this arid plain of round pebbles could be transformed into rolling grasslands. All that was needed was water. Accordingly, in the 16th century, Adam de Craponne commissioned the building of an irrigation canal whose waters were to make the Crau bloom, and give Salon its distinctive pastoral setting of olive groves and meadows.

At the foot of the **Porte de l'Horloge** (Clock Gate), crowned by a belfry, the **Fontaine Moussue** (Mossy Fountain) murmurs quietly as it spills its watery pearls. Nearby, **Nostradamus' House** is now a museum. **Saint Michael's Church** is Romanesque. One of its two bell towers, a 13th century arcaded tower, lends the church a wonderful airiness. Its remarkable sculptured tympanum shows the Archangel Michael, wrapped in fat, supple-bodied serpents, below a timid and astonished Pascal Lamb, amid a stylised decor of leaves and flowers. Stairs lead from the old market square to **Empéri Castle**, which, balanced at the top of Puech Rock, overshadows the town. Once the property of the bishops of Arles, the castle was converted into barracks in the 19th century. Today, it houses the Empéri Museum, a museum of military art and history where the collections of Raoul and Jean Brunon are displayed. **Saint Lawrence's Collegiate Church** is a fine example of Provençal Gothic achitecture. A recent epitaph pays homage to the famous astrologer, Nostradamus, whose prophecies captivate his readers even today, at the end of the 20th century.

A Man Named Michel de Notre-Dame

It was in 1555 that Michel de Notre-Dame, also known as Michel de Nostre-Dame, published his prophetic tome, *Astrological Centuries*, as Nostradamus. The author, whose name is not so much a poor Latinisation of his surname as a play on words meaning "we give what belongs to us", was born in Saint-Rémy-de-Provence and moved to Salon after his marriage in 1547. As a physician seeking to improve the then rather limited efficacy of medical practice, he began exploring the realms of astrology in search of cures and miracles. Qualified as supernatural, even diabolical, his mystical ways aroused much interest among his contemporaries, and many illustrious visitors, including Catherine de Médicis and her son, Charles IX, consulted him in person. His collection of enigmatic quatrain verse, *Centuries*, so skillfully written that anyone could read into it just what they wished, was, naturally, an immediate success. But can it really be said to hold the key to the future, when its esoteric language can be understood only by reviewing events in the light of hindsight, and its obscure predictions validated only by stretching historical fact to fit? But, while the mystery remains, one thing is certain: on July 2nd, 1566, the great seer died.

Salon: Nostradamus' epitaph

Aix-en-Provence

Rarely does a town manage to reconcile so successfully its historical past, carefully preserving the remains of earlier days when glory and elegance went hand in hand, with the demands of a busy, modern urban community. But Aix-en-Provence, sprinkled with fountains, simply blossoms, its golden heart swelling with the sunny memories that infuse each of its ancient stones, its suburbs opening like petals into spreading outskirts, then merging gently into the surrounding hazy countryside.

It was, in fact, *Massalia*, the Greek city of Marseilles, that was responsible for founding the Roman town of *Aquæ Sextiæ*. In the 2nd century B.C., Rome, allied with Marseilles, had just conquered Spain. But the land routes between Rome and the Iberian Peninsula, from the Ligurian coast to the Pyrenees, were so insecure that, when threatened by their common enemy, the Salian Franks, the Roman Senate didn't hesitate to come to *Massalia*'s aid. At the time, the Salians occupied the inland regions around the Phocaean port and, from their solid oppidum at Entremont, had turned their greedy gaze towards the nearby coast. In 125 B.C., the Roman troops crossed the Alps and, the following year, the Proconsul Sextius Calvinus decided it was time to crush the Salians. They put up a fierce fight, but their spirit was finally broken when, with the ferocity of a victor who has feared a former foe too much to allow him the slightest chance of recovery, Calvinus razed their capital, Entremont, to the ground, leaving nothing but ruins. Knowing that the wounds left by such destruction needed to be healed without delay, Calvinus resolved to build an urban centre which would capture the interest, and perhaps even temper the high spirits, of the local population.

Great care was taken in choosing the site: on the plain (the heights being too inhospitable), at the crossroads of what were to become Roman roads (parts of the *Via Aurelia* still exist to prove it), and where warm, health-giving, freshwater springs rose to the surface. The omens were good, the gods seemed to smile, and, with no more ado, *Aquæ Sextiæ* – named, as the Greek geographer, Strabon, noted, after its waters and its originator – was founded.

But the *castellum* of *Aquæ Sextiæ* hadn't done with violence yet and, when the Cimbri and Teutone tribes appeared on the horizon, it set about resisting the would-be invaders with what it hoped would be greater efficiency than that shown by the unhappy *Arausio* (Orange). That skillful and courageous soldier, the Consul Marius, was brought in with orders to stop the barbarians before they took the road to Italy. At the head of five legions, he set up camp in southern Gaul and patiently awaited the coming conflict. When the Teutones crossed the Durance and began moving southeast, Marius, a clever strategist, followed at a distance before engaging them in action. Although the exact site of the battle, which took place in 102 B.C., is the subject of some conjecture, it was probably the little valley of the Torse, tributary of the Arc, that echoed with the furious clamour of the fight. Perhaps the Greek writer, Plutarch, exaggerated when he recorded 100,000 enemy dead, but the memory of this Roman victory over the dreaded Germans is still so fresh in the collective Provençal mind that, even today, the name of Marius represents all that is truly Provence!

To begin with, Aix-en-Provence was a Latin colony, and the civil rights of its inhabitants were recognised by Rome. Later, Augustus accorded it the far greater honour of admitting it to the tightly closed ranks of the Roman *civitas*, or city-states, and its population became Roman citizens. For three long centuries, Aix was at peace. The ancient remains displayed in the Granet Museum give some idea of the prosperity enjoyed at that time, as, in contrast to the strange severed heads of the Entremont trophies, they tell of life in a quiet Roman city. It was only much later, in the 13th century, under Charles of Anjou, brother of Saint Louis, that Aix-en-Provence become that elegant city so dear to the hearts of the Counts of Provence. Later still, in the 15th century, King René established his court here, transforming Aix into one of the finest capitals of Europe.

But when Provence became part of the kingdom of France in 1482, Aix-en-Provence, in spite of its Parliament, was no more than a provincial town. Then, towards the end of the 16th century, a new class of wealthy magistrates began to emerge and Aix prospered once more. These learned men of law built luxurious mansions, fountains in the public squares, and wide avenues for their fine carriages and coaches. It was here that the colourful and capricious Honoré Gabriel Riqueti, Count of Mirabeau, got into endless trouble, shamelessly seducing Aix's innocent young women. Repeated stays in the royal prisons of If and Vincennes Castles, far from calming him down, brought him to reflect on the evils of despotism and determine to fight it. When the States General met in 1789 and he was elected to the Third Estate, Mirabeau, with all his strengths and weaknesses, became one of the key figures of the French Revolution.

At Aix's very heart lies the **Cours Mirabeau**. Lined with fine mansions and dotted with fountains, this avenue runs under a leafy tunnel in a perfectly straight line. Spilling its warm waters in veils of fine mist, the **Fontaine Moussue** is, as its name implies, covered in moss. At one end of this lively thoroughfare, Good King René proudly bears a bunch of the fat Muscat grapes that owe him their fame, while, at the other, the fountains of the **Rotonde** gush enthusiastically. A gentle stroll through the old winding streets towards Saint Saviour's Cathedral is the best way to admire some of Aix's *hôtels particuliers*, or **private mansions**. Some, such as the Hôtel Caumont and the Hôtel Maynier d'Oppède draw the inspiration for their soberly elegant facades from Classical architecture. Others, such as the Hôtel d'Albertas, spread around courtyards so vast that they have become public squares. Still

others, such as the Hôtel d'Agut, whose wide portal is graced by a pair of Atlantean figures, inspired by the Puget school, burst with barely contained baroque exuberance.

Drunk on the heady perfumes distilled by the flower market in the hot Provençal sun, the **Tour de l'Horloge** (Clock Tower) once assured Aix's protection. Today, its tocsin bell, shut up in its wrought iron belfry, still sounds the hour and marks the changing seasons. Nearby, the high facades of the **Hôtel de Ville** (Town Hall) frame a splendid square tower.

Set among the white stone buildings through which Rue Gaston-de-Saporta picks its way, the **Cathédrale Saint-Sauveur** (Saint Sav-

Good King René

In 1434, René, younger son of Louis II of Anjou, inherited the County of Provence. Like his illustrious predecessors, however, René felt drawn irresistibly towards Naples and Sicily, whose rightful king he claimed to be. It was only much later, after repeated defeats in Campania, that an older and wiser René at last turned his gaze towards Provence. And what he saw delighted him so much that he decided to settle his court permanently in Aix-en-Provence. René – who was polyglot, being fluent even in Hebrew, scholarly, knowing astrology and mathematics, and skilled in the use of both calligrapher's pen and illuminator's paintbrush – became the legendary "Good King René" and Provence prospered under the influence of its modern sovereign. Cleanliness and hygiene became the bywords of its capital, Aix-en-Provence, and his vineyards at Gardanne yielded their new wonder, the Muscat grape, and – even though the court's expenditure weighed the little paradise down under an increasingly heavy burden of taxation – Provence, under René and his young queen, Jeanne, experienced its golden age.

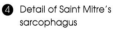

Aix-en-Provence: Saint Saviour's Cathedral -

1 The cloisters

2 One of the door panels

3 The baptistry

4 Detail of Saint Mitre's sarcophagus

The Tapestry Museum:

5 Scene from the life of Don Quixote

iour's Cathedral) is Aix's true pride and joy. Protected by heavy shutters, the panels of its door, sculptured in the 16th century by Jean Guiramand, show the four prophets surrounded by twelve sibyls. At the risk of compromising its architectural purity, the cathedral has collected souvenirs from each period that marked its history. There is a Roman *cardo*, an open reminder of a very pagan past, a Merovingian baptistry, set unself-consciously in a magnificent ring of Roman columns, an elegantly sober Romanesque nave, dedicated to Saint Maxim, where Saint Mitre's long sarcophagus lies, and, finally, a central Gothic nave which lends the cathedral fullness and volume. The triptych of the *Burning Bush* was painted in 1476 by that great artist of Aix's royal court, Nicolas Froment. With a *Madonna and Child* on the central panel, its outer panels show Good King René and his queen, Jeanne de Laval, kneeling in prayer. The 12th century cloisters, with a timber roof instead of a vaulted ceiling, open in fine colonnades.

Aix boasts a number of other churches worthy of note. Its high bell tower cleaving the clear skies, the austerely Gothic **Saint-Jean-de-Malte** (Saint John of Malta's Church) was the burial place of the Counts of Provence. Behind a Classical facade, the **Eglise de la Madeleine** (Church of the Magdalene) is suffused by the youthful grace of an 18th century marble *Virgin Mary*, so lively and light that she almost seems to dance, and by the serene splendour of a 15th century triptych of the *Annunciation*.

In the past, the archbishops of Aix played a leading role in the town's government. Their palace, the **Archevêché**, was built between the mid 17th century and 1730. Its courtyard has since been renovated and equipped to stage the theatrical and, more especially, the musical events that mark Aix's famous annual festival. The palace also houses the Tapestry Museum whose fine Beauvais tapestries – including the *Grotesques*, telling the fabulous tale of Don Quixote, and *Les Jeux Russiens*, showing rural games – illustrate a wide variety of themes.

Aix-en-Provence: Saint Saviour's Cathedral - The triptych of the *Burning Bush*

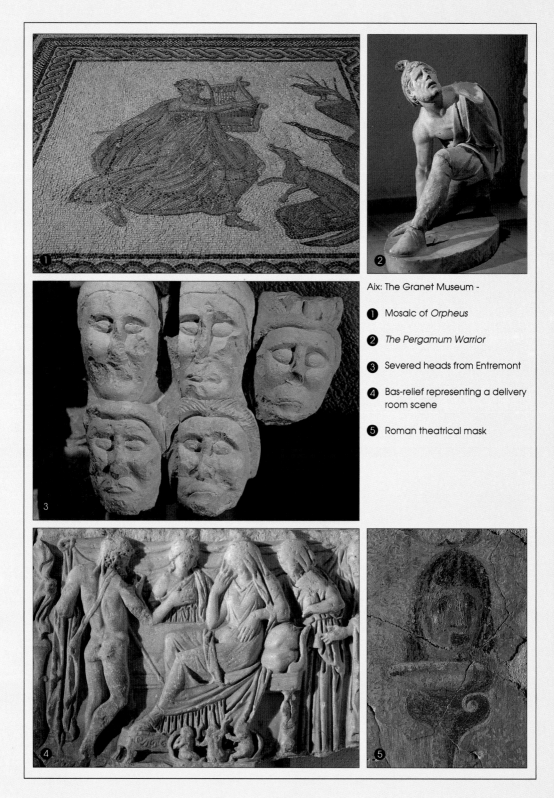

Aix: The Granet Museum -

1 Mosaic of *Orpheus*

2 *The Pergamum Warrior*

3 Severed heads from Entremont

4 Bas-relief representing a delivery room scene

5 Roman theatrical mask

The Granet Museum

In the 18th century, on the initiative of certain masters who wished to associate the teaching of art more closely with the works of the great artists of the past, the faculty of arts of the University of Provence created the "Chambers of Antiquities and Paintings", assembling a number of fine art collections. Known until 1949 as the Museum of Aix, the Granet Museum, housed, since 1829, in the former priory of the Knights of Malta, took over these different collections and improved them. François Granet, born in Aix-en-Provence in 1775, was curator of the royal museums. At his death in 1849, his work – canvases depicting monastic life and Provençal landscapes – was added to the existing collections, and in 1949, the museum's name was changed in his honour. The Granet Museum houses representative works from all schools of painting – Byzantine, Flemish, Dutch, Italian, French and Provençal – which, from the 14th century Byzantine triptychs to the luminous works of Cézanne, provide an exhaustive overview of the history of art. But the Granet Museum also boasts a particularly rich archeological collection. With one knee to the ground and a movingly anxious look in his eye, *The Pergamum Warrior* bears all the hallmarks of the works produced by the Greek school of Asia Minor in the 2nd century B.C.. Most of the pieces displayed come from the region's two main archeological sites, the oppidum of Entremont and the Roman town of *Aquæ Sextiæ*. The solid torso of a warrior, clad in a breastplate, the strange series of stacked heads, and, in particular, the bas-relief of a horseman with his head severed, are important examples of Celtic-Ligurian art. Finally, numerous pottery items, mosaics, bas-reliefs and paintings recall the fact that Aix-en-Provence was once a great Gallo-Roman city.

Horseman with severed head

1 Roquefavour Aqueduct

2 Joseph Sec's Mausoleum

3 Pioline Castle

4 Le Tholonet Castle

5 Vauvenargues Castle

Around Aix-en-Provence

Silhouetted against the clear Provençal sky, **Roquefavour Aqueduct** is remarkable both as a fine feat of engineering and for the solemn beauty of its three rows of arches that carry the waters of the Durance towards Marseilles.

Provence's *bastides* date from the pre-revolutionary days of the *Ancien Régime*. Set among expanses of open grounds, with drives, bowed under leafy tunnels, that sweep away towards views of ornamental lakes and the murmuring fountains of rotundas, the **Château de la Pioline** is typical of this kind of country mansion built during the golden age of the aristocracy.

Joseph Sec's Mausoleum was built in 1792 by a joiner from Aix-en-Provence as his contribution to the revolutionary movement.

To the north of Aix, the **Entremont Plateau** was the site of a prosperous Celtic-Ligurian oppidum long before the elegant *Aquæ Sextiæ* was founded. In the upper town, which bristles with ramparts, stone houses line regularly laid-out streets. The lower town, built to a less organised plan, was probably the craftsmen's and traders' district since, among the finds made there, is the stone from an oil press. The wide sculptured portico is worthy of note, although its exact purpose remains a mystery. The heavy fortifications with regularly spaced round towers that surround the lower town indicate that, even in those early days, the art of fortifying towns was developing hand-in-hand with the poliorcetic one of besieging them.

Falling in love with **Vauvenargues Castle**, Pablo Picasso made it his home, and was even buried here, under the hot Provençal sun, in the middle of the castle's terrace.

It is not only the 18th century castle with its regular facade and its geometric gardens that make **Le Tholonet** so charming a site. A short walk, and the jagged walls of a very ancient Roman dam can be seen, recalling the remarkable perseverance the Romans applied to solving the problem of providing fresh water.

Le Tholonet: The Roman dam

Mont Sainte-Victoire

Buttressed by the nearly perfect arc of the Cengle Mountain, Mont Sainte-Victoire keeps faithful watch over Aix-en-Provence. Its dazzling whiteness betrays its limestone heart as it rises clean and clear against the azure skies, shaped by the relentless forces of erosion into a crouching monster's spine. The origin of its name is something of a mystery. The persistent memory of that famous victory won by the Roman General Marius, or, and perhaps more probably, the etymological derivative of the name of some Celtic-Ligurian god? Both theories stand; neither can be proved. From the foot of the cross, the *Croix de Provence*, on the summit of a rocky ridge, the horizon opens up in a perfect circle.

Blending into the rock, the tiny chapel of Saint Ser's Hermitage hides, in the heart of its apse, the little cave where the good hermit spent his days, cut off from the world of men.

Cézanne

Right in front of him, within easy reach of his palette, was the most compliant, and yet the most capricious, of all artists' models – Mont Sainte-Victoire. And, on some sixty different occasions, setting his blank canvas purposefully before him, Cézanne attempted, tirelessly, to capture the light and the rhythm, both flowing and halting, of this grandiose landscape. Skillfully laying down impressions of shape and hue in bold brushstrokes of solid colour, and dispensing with lines and shadows, he retained no more than a symphony of tones: dark purple and jade skies, curious mixtures of greens blended to black, and mosaics of orange, crackling with heat. And even now, sometimes, when the mood is right, Sainte-Victoire once more miraculously transforms itself into a Cézanne painting.

Mont Sainte-Victoire: Saint Ser's Hermitage

AROUND THE SAINTE-BAUME MASSIF

Saint-Maximin-la-Sainte-Baume

At the edge of the plain, beyond the place where the narrow parallel rows of the Var vineyards converge, the imposing form of Sainte-Marie-Madeleine's Basilica rises majestically above a broken line of rooftops, catching the last rays of the setting sun. With no fine stone tower or spire-topped belfry, it is the sheer size and volume of this building that make it so remarkable. Built in the late 13th century, the basilica lies at the very heart of the community and provides the town with its true *raison d'être*. With its streets laid out in a regular grid, fountains singing in its squares, and strong ramparts – now disappeared – Saint-Maximin-la-Sainte-Baume was once a typical medieval *ville neuve*, or bastide. It only remained for Charles II of Anjou to discover, or, rather, invent, the tombs of Saint Mary Magdalene and Saint Maximinus and to commission building of the basilica, for this quiet hamlet to become a beautiful town and host to many illustrious pilgrims. The Gothic period graced the basilica with airy vaults set on clusters of pillars, while Provençal architecture left its distinctive mark of sobriety and light. And the Provençal skies give shape and form to the basilica's volumes, as their soft blue brightness streaming through the long windows of the apse bathes the nave in a gentle heavenly glow. As the centuries passed, each left its stamp on the basilica's decor. The 16th century altarpiece of the Passion, painted by Antoine Ronzen in 1520, consists of twenty-two paint-

Saint-Maximin-la-Sainte-Baume: Sainte-Marie-Madeleine's Basilica

ings, depicting Christ on the cross surrounded by the strait-laced figures of the saints. The 17th century choir stalls, with their backs of sculptured medallions, are exceptionally fine. Carved, then polished to perfection, the wood gently twists, curves and swells, shining with a tawny glow. Not to be outdone, the 18th century gave the basilica a fine pulpit, wrapped in a spiral staircase, under a triumphantly spreading canopy. Sculptured in 1756 by Louis Gudet, it is one of the finest pieces of the basilica's renowned collection of furnishings. Coaxed by the artist's skillful fingers, the countless pipes of the organ, commissioned by Brother Isnard in 1773, can modulate delicate chords of crystal purity, or reverberate with the echoes of the tempest's clamour.

The crypt is a burial chamber, housing the 5th century sarcophagi of Saint Magdalene, Saint Marcella, Saint Maximinus and Saint Sidoine. Surrounded by monastic buildings, the cloisters of the royal convent open onto a jumble of boxwood, lime, cedar and cypress trees.

Mary Magdalene

Mary of Magdala – that celebrated sinner who responded to the call of Christ – was there as her Lord was led to be crucified and sweetened the last moments of his life with her tears. Later, that legendary little boat brought her, with the other Mary, Martha, Lazarus, Maximinus, and Sarah, to Saintes-Maries-de-la-Mer. From there, she went on to the dark *baume*, or cave, at the heart of the massif, where, for thirty years, she lived a solitary life of prayer until the angels, filled with pity, wrapped her in their wings and took her to Saint-Maximin-la-Sainte-Baume where she breathed her last. And so began the strange peregrinations of her relics. Buried, forgotten, stolen, and finally miraculously rediscovered by Charles of Anjou, Count of Provence, they became the finest jewel in the little town's crown.

Saint-Maximin: Detail of the choir stalls

Saint-Maximin: The cloisters of the royal convent

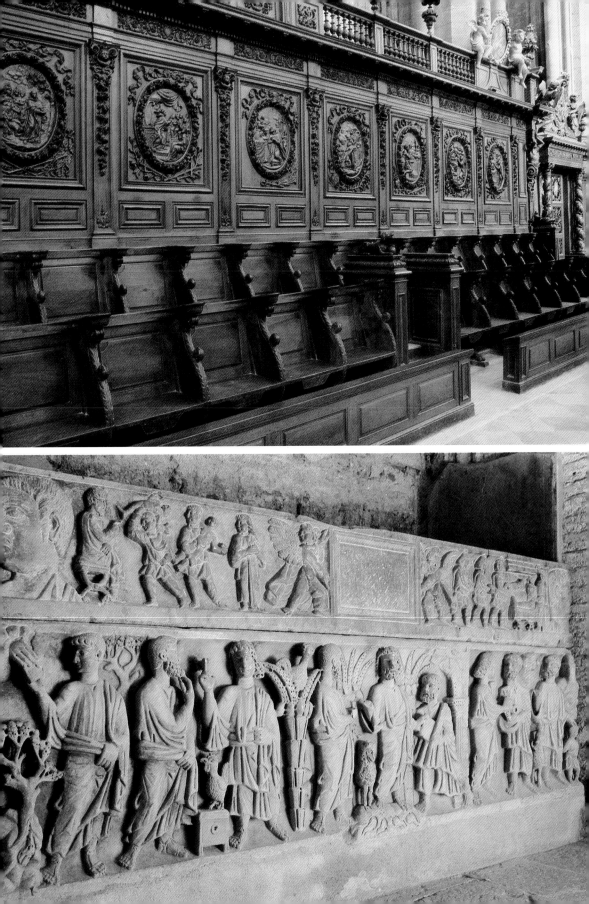

1 Barjols: A fountain

2 Saint-Julien-le-Montagnier:
The church

3 Saint-Martin-de-Pallières

To the North of Saint-Maximin-la-Sainte-Baume

The solid dovecote at **Brue-Auriac** watches benignly over the road to **Barjols**, perched on top of the *colline jolie* – the pretty hill – from which the town gets its name. Mossy fountains gently murmuring in its shady squares make Barjols a very pleasant place indeed. The 11th century collegiate church of Notre-Dame-des-Epines, now Notre-Dame-de-l'Assomption, has been extensively rebuilt over the years: its cloisters have disappeared and a delicate 18th century belfry added to its bell tower. The castle at **Saint-Martin-de-Pallières** overshadows the village and its 17th century church. One of the most precious parts of the ramparts that once encircled **Saint-Julien-le-Montagnier** – the monumental gate of the Knights Templars – is still there to be admired, and the village's 13th century church still boasts a number of Carolingian features.

Brue-Auriac: The dovecote

The Sainte-Baume Massif

Both mountain and forest have seized upon the name *baume* (the Provençal word for *cave*), quite unashamedly laying claim to the well-established fame of the legendary and holy retreat of Mary Magdalene who, redeemed by divine grace, came here, to this grandiose landscape, to seek the solitude of repentance.

As Alps and Pyrenees, slowly but surely, undertook the lengthy business of mountain building, the great orogenic upheavals of the Tertiary era were not to leave these sedimentary strata unmoved. Their heavy layers of limestone and marl buckled and folded, and sometimes, when the pressure became too great, even broke and were lifted up into vertical rocky ridges. Born of these movements of the earth's crust, Sainte-Baume, like Sainte-Victoire, is characterised by the astonishing dissymmetry of its opposite faces. To the south, the limestone bed rises in a gentle slope where strips of stony ground and rough garrigue blaze with sun-burnt colour. Nothing on this southern side warns of the sudden vertical white cliffs of the northern face, below which lie the first rolling stretches of the Aups Plateau, hidden under the soft and leafy canopy of the Sainte-Baume National Forest. Dampness and freshness are the distinctive features of this north-facing side which lies, overwhelmed, in the thick, unmoving shadow of the towering cliff. The walk through the forest of oak, lime and maple towards that famous cave – Mary Magdalene's legendary retreat – is pure delight, and the climb to the chapel that stands on the summit of Saint-Pilon brings with it the strange sensation of somehow rising above the baser, more material, considerations of everyday life.

The ruins of **Saint Pons' Abbey**, once a Cistercian convent, lie hidden among magnificent grounds where, muffled by soft mossy cushions, the gentle murmuring of cool fountains can just be discerned.

The Sainte-Baume Massif: The grounds of Saint Pons' Abbey - A waterfall

Aubagne

Overshadowed by Garlaban Rock, Aubagne lies in a natural basin between the Huveaune and the Merlançon. In Roman times, *Albinia* – the white town – was already a busy market place. Potters are known to have worked here as early as the 16th century, and, ever since the Revolution, Aubagne's *santon* makers have peopled their traditional Christmas Cribs with characters drawn from Provençal society. In their miniaturized world, the *Petit Monde de Marcel Pagnol*, they pay homage to their fellow countryman, the famous writer, born here in 1895. The French Foreign Legion has been based in Aubagne since 1962 and the museum at Camp Viénot celebrates the outstanding courage of these soldiers who have fought in every major combat of recent French history. Not far from there, **Saint-Jean-de-Garguier's Chapel** houses a collection of ex-votos, dating from the 15th century to modern times.

Marcel Pagnol

When, in 1957, Marcel Pagnol chose to set *La Gloire de Mon Père* (published in English in 1960 with *Le Château de Ma Mère*, as *The Days Were Too Short*) in the country of his own childhood – in the heart of the garrigue – the Garlaban, the Taoumé, Grosibou Cave and Buzine Castle, coming to life under his pen, all became places of legend. His characters portray humankind so naturally and so spontaneously that they become moving archetypes – caricatures almost – living in a blessed world full of generosity and humorous wisdom. And, while César exchanges grumbling rejoinders with Mr. Panisse and Mr. Brun in the Old Port of Marseilles, Manon, Angèle, Naïs and Fanny still blossom with the freshness of youth, whose intrigues are woven with love, honour and dignity.

The *Petit Monde de Pagnol: The Card Game*

The *Petit Monde de Pagnol: Playing Pétanque*

Aubagne: The Foreign Legion War Memorial

3

MARSEILLES AND ITS COAST

From Cape Canaille to the Gates of Marseilles

To the southeast of the fishing village, seaside resort and residential area of Cassis (whatever you do, if you don't want to upset the locals, don't pronounce the last *s* in its name), the coastal road, the Route des Crêtes, climbs the Saoupe Mountain to Cape Canaille, heedless of the dizzy heights of the Soubeyran Cliffs, the highest in France. To the west, accessible only by rough footpath or by sea, the *calanques*, or coastal inlets, remain havens of unspoilt beauty. It was movements in the earth's crust which, long ago, folded layers of sedimentary rocks into stony mountain ranges, narrow limestone ridges and steep-sided canyons. Channeled inescapably into these passages, rivers and streams carved their valleys deeper still as they reached down to sea level, which, in the days of the Quaternary glaciation period, was much lower than it is today. As the climate became milder, the glaciers began to melt and the seas to rise. The deep river valleys were flooded and the *calanques*, or "Mediterranean fjords", were formed. Their names are as soft as their limpid waters: Port-Miou, Port-Pin, En-Vau, Sugiton, Morgiou and Sormiou. It was while diving in the latter in 1991, that Henri Cosquer discovered a cave, thirty-seven metres below sea level. Its walls are covered with paintings: negative hands some 27,000 years old, with horses, bison, seals and penguins carved onto the rock or outlined in black more than 17,000 years ago.

Cassis: The harbour

Morgiou Inlet

From east to west, the foothills of the Puget and Marseilleveyre Hills stretch their rocky ridges as far as Cape Croisette. From the Callelongue Inlet, the road climbs back up towards Marseilles, passing through La Madrague-de-Montredon, the Pointe-Rouge Marina and, at the tiny mouth of the Huveaune, Prado Beach. Next to Prado Beach, Borély Park, with its fifty-five hectares of grounds and, to the south, its castle, features both French and English styles of gardening and boasts one of the finest rose gardens in Europe.

At the point where the coastal road, the President J. F. Kennedy Corniche, overhangs the sheer drop to Marseilles harbour, there is a magnificent view across the bay to the islands, scattered haphazardly among short curling waves, and bathed in soft blue light. Leaving the coast behind for a while, the road plunges into the jumble of narrow streets of the Endoume district, before emerging at the Vallon des Auffes where colourful lines of fishing boats lie moored along the quays.

Marseilles: The Vallon des Auffes

Marseilles: Prado Beach

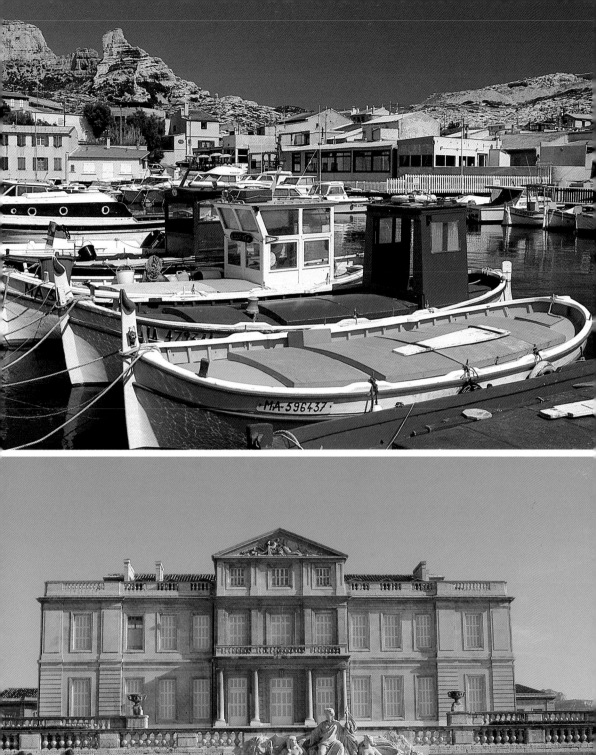

Marseilles

Traces of a very ancient Celtic-Ligurian civilisation, dating back as far as the first millennium B.C., have been found in the region between the Rhone and the Var. These tribes were almost certainly the ancestors of the Salians, whose settlements were grouped around their capital on the heights of Entremont. The coast, visited by the bold seafaring peoples of the eastern Mediterranean, was, at the time, occupied only sporadically. Over a long period, the enterprising Phocaeans explored the sea. Forced by the limited navigational skills of their day, and their knowledge of the stars, to stay within sight of land, and constantly in search of outlets for their business ambitions, they kept close to the coastline. Sailing by the site of present-day Marseilles, around the year 700 B.C., they discovered white cliffs plunging into foaming indigo seas, tiny sheltered sandy crescents in hidden inlets, and a wide harbour, providing deep anchorage, set between hills that watched over a scattered group of small islands, just a few *stadions* from the shore. Feeling immediately at home in this Aegean setting, the Phocaeans disembarked and established a trading post here which, by the year 600 B.C., had developed into the Greek colony of *Massalia*. Today, a stroll through the **Jardin des Vestiges** – the Garden of Ruins – to the quays of the ancient port, now caressed by fresh green waves of lawn, conjures up visions of ancient galleys bobbing gently on the surf. In those days, before the land had been painstakingly separated from the waters, the mouth of the Lacydon was lost among marshes. Wary of the sea, source of all dangers, the Greeks protected themselves by building solid ramparts. Given the importance of the archeological finds made in the Bourse (stock exchange) district, in 1972, the town of Marseilles created the **Musée d'Histoire** – the History Museum. From the Roquepertuse Portico to the exhibi-

tion of ancient ship building methods, pieced together in the minutest detail from the extraordinary remains of a Roman merchant vessel, discovered in 1974, the museum helps its visitors better understand the ancient town and fully enjoy its many treasures. Peaceful and prosperous, the Greek city of *Massalia* was governed by six hundred *timouques*, or wealthy merchant citizens, and remained faithful to its very Greek gods, Apollo of Delphi and Artemis of Ephesus. Keeping both their religious practices and their language free from any local influence, the inhabitants of *Massalia*, far from denying their Phocaean origins, openly publicised them. In the third century B.C., du-

When Gyptis Met Protis...

The legend of the founding of Marseilles, as told by the 2nd century Roman historian, Justin, is a tale of true love. The Phocaean fleet had just dropped anchor in a marshy harbour. The journey had been difficult, but the leaders of the expedition, Simos and the handsome Protis, were quick to realise the potential of the site. All they had to do was meet the king of these lands and, having courted his friendship, build a port worthy of their considerable seafaring capacities. Nann, King of the Segobriges, and master of the region, was very busy, having organised a banquet in honour of his daughter, the sweet Gyptis, during which she was to choose her husband. The festivities were in full swing when the two Greek heroes, welcomed as friends, were invited to join the party. All her suitors were there, agitated and anxious, but Protis was as handsome as one of Phidias' statues of the Greek gods and Gyptis couldn't take her eyes off him. At last, she made her choice, and raised her cup of clear water to this gentle-eyed foreigner. After which, all the young couple had to do was to found *Massalia* and live happily ever after!

ring the Second Punic War, *Massalia* and Rome joined forces against their common enemy, Carthage. Their alliance seemed so sound that Marseilles, troubled by the ever increasing threat posed by the turbulent Gauls, quite naturally called upon Rome's efficient legions to re-establish order. Unable to resist so attractive an invitation, the Romans gladly seized the opportunity to establish a foothold in transalpine Gaul, and *Massalia* became a Greek enclave on an increasingly Roman coastline. The balance of power between the two was delicate, but stable, so long as the inhabitants of *Massalia* kept out of Rome's internal quarrels. When the ambitious Pompey and Caesar became locked in their power struggle, Marseilles, underestimating the implacable Caesar, sided with Pompey. The revenge of the victorious Caesar was terrible. In 49 B.C., after six months of siege, *Massalia* fell to the Romans, and the days of brilliant Greek reasoning, lucrative trade, independence and freedom were over. Crushed and ransacked, the city lost its fleet and its trading posts, and was absorbed into the Roman world, although, as witnessed by the rows of enormous pottery jars or *dolia*, used for storing oil, wine and grain, and now preserved *in situ* in the **Roman Docks Museum**, it remained a busy port.

Influenced by the spread of Christianity throughout the Empire, Marseilles, according to legend, had its very own martyr: a certain Victor. This rather obscure character, condemned to death in the late 3rd century by the Emperor Maximian, became the patron saint of **Saint Victor's Abbey**, founded by Cassian in the 5th century. The church – guardian of the port – with curtain walls, fortified towers and crenellations, is every inch a fortress. In the 11th century, a new church was built, and the 5th century basilica, which houses a series of antique and Paleo-Christian sarcophagi, was buried in the maze of its foundations. The tombstone of the Catalan monk, Isarn, who built the 11th century church, is located in one of the crypts leading to the cave sanctuaries.

For centuries, Marseilles' trading activity was concentrated in the charming **Vieux-Port**, or Old Port, which, echoing to the sound of the local lilting accent, was closely guarded by its twin forts, Saint John's and Saint Nicholas'. The spongy marshland soils at the back of the inlet were particularly well-suited to growing hemp, which, after a long transformation process, provided ropes and rigging for the sailing boats anchored in the port. The area used to grow the hemp, the *chènevière*, gave its name to Marseilles' most famous thoroughfare, the **Canebière**. Sadly, the building of this avenue – worthy of any built in Paris by Haussmann – and other 19th century developments, left **Saint Ferréol's Church** disfigured and the architectural harmony of its exterior destroyed.

The **Musée du Vieux-Marseille** is housed in the 16th century Maison Diamantée, named after the diamond-shaped stones of its facade which create a many-faceted decor of light and shade. Currently closed to the public, the museum boasts a delightful collection of period

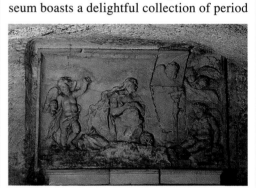
Marseilles: Saint Victor's Abbey - A bas-relief

Marseilles: The Canebière

1 The Roman Docks Museum:
   An anchor

2 The Roman Docks Museum:
   Supporting wall and storage jars

3 Saint John's Fort

4 Saint Victor's Basilica: *The
   Innocent Saints' Sarcophagus*

Marseilles:

❶ The Grobet-Labadié Museum:
A Gobelins tapestry - *Winter*

❷ The Archeological Museum:
A funeral urn

❸ The Archeological Museum:
A large Greek *puxis*

❹ The Grobet-Labadié Museum:
Primitive Italian painting

costumes, where padded fabrics, or *boutis*, lend softness and volume to brightly coloured petticoats, and where ladies' *frégate* (frigate) headdresses, with their incredibly fine lace and the airy gathers of their voluminous starched flounces, rival one another in boldness. One room is dedicated to the great plague of 1720. Laden with the riches of the east, a merchant ship from Syria arrived in Marseilles' harbour. Eager to get to the great fair at Beaucaire, Marseilles' rich traders hurried to unload their merchandise, and, in their haste, released the ship's terrible, and as yet, undeclared, stowaway – the plague. Sickness and death swept through the town at such an astonishing rate that the galley slaves, charged with the unenviable task of burying the dead, couldn't work fast enough and the streets were littered with thousands of bodies. Spreading throughout Provence, the epidemic claimed 100,000 victims – a heavy toll indeed for a brief moment's financial gain. The Camoin Room, named after an 18th century playing card manufacturer, pays tribute to this flourishing industry with displays of tools, lithographic stones, ace-shaped stencils and decks of the famous Marseilles tarot cards. Nearby, the typically 17th century facade of the Hôtel de Ville – the Town Hall – bears the Sun King's coat of arms.

The **Centre de la Vieille-Charité**, a former charity hospice, built by Marseilles' baroque artist, Pierre Puget, houses the collections of the Mediterranean and Egyptian Archeological Museum, recently moved from Borély Castle.

The **Cantini Museum** provides a quality showcase for cubism and surrealism, representational and non-representational styles alike.

Inaugurated in 1926, the **Grobet-Labadié Museum** houses the collections bequeathed to the city of Marseilles by the Grobet-Labadié family, and reveals the eclecticism and fine taste of these traders turned patrons of the arts. Among the 5,000 pieces on display are collections of faience (glazed earthenware) and antique instruments, a large number of drawings, and some fine 18th century furniture.

The Archeological Museum: Glazed earthenware lion

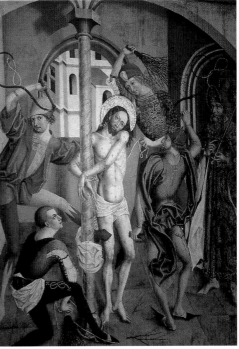

The Grobet-Labadié Museum: Dutch school

213

In the 19th century, as trade developed hand-in-hand with the building of France's colonial empire in Africa, great monuments, as only the gifted engineers of that century knew how to build, began to spring up in Marseilles. Crowning the 162-metre high rocky needle that dominates Marseilles, **Notre-Dame-de-la-Garde**, built by Jacques Henri Espérandieu, marries the Romanesque and Byzantine styles of architecture. Topped by a huge gilt statue of the *Madona and Child*, and covered in mosaics and ex-votos, the basilica became the symbol of that *Bonne Mère*, or Good Mother, whose name is so often invoked by the people of Marseilles. Another giant of the same style, **Sainte-Marie-Majeure's Cathedral**, with its exuberant striped facade, outshines the very soberly elegant Old Major, part of which was sacrificed to build the new edifice. Linked by a neoclassical Ionic colonnade over a cascading fountain, the twin wings of **Longchamp Palace**, also of the 19th century, house the Fine Arts and Natural History Museums.

Marseilles: The New Major

A work by Puget

Marseilles: Longchamp Palace

If Castle

Some places owe their fame more to the fiction of legend and literature than to the facts of their own history. If Castle, shrouded in an aura of mystery, is a typical example of this phenomenon. Edmond Dantès, the hero of Alexandre Dumas' famous novel, *The Count of Monte Cristo*, was imprisoned here for fourteen long years. Capable of performing the most improbable of daring deeds, he even managed to escape the confines of this, the most secure of all prisons.

But If Castle was not always a prison. Having just suffered the naval attacks launched against Marseilles by his enemy and rival, the Emperor Charles V, King François I decided to counter the future possibility of any similar such offensives by building a fortress on one of the small rocky islands of the Frioul Archipelago. And, in just four years, between 1524 and 1528, If Castle was completed.

At the end of the 16th century, the castle, considered too vulnerable, began to bristle with new fortifications: curtain walls, watch towers and bastions. Designed to withstand lengthy sieges, the fortress was equipped to survive entirely cut off from the outside world, with adequate supplies of water, food and ammunition. With the political stability of the 17th century, the castle's defensive role became somewhat superfluous. Consequently, in 1634, it was transformed into a royal prison and its defences, designed initially to keep the enemy out, became insurmountable obstacles ideal for keeping all manner of prisoners – including the enigmatic Man in the Iron Mask – in.

Just a stone's throw away, the islands of **Pomègues** and **Ratonneau**, part of the same archipelago, once served as lazarettos. As an essential preventative measure designed to protect the mainland from the risk of major epidemics, the victims of contagious disease were kept there in isolation for forty days at a time, while their health was monitored.

If Castle: The courtyard and cells

The Estaque Chain

Along this narrow rocky limestone ridge, tectonic and erosive forces have lent themselves wholeheartedly to the task of complicating what would otherwise be a relief of insignificant proportions. Although its highest point doesn't even reach an altitude of 300 metres, crossing the rocky slopes of the Estaque Chain is still quite a remarkable feat. Isolated for years from the rest of the world, and inhabited only by the goats of Le Rove – famed for their fragrant soft cheese, called *brousse* – the region was at last opened up in the 19th century, as revolutionary engineering advances made it possible to cut across the rough surface of this arid limestone ridge and pierce its very heart. A rail tunnel, a coastal railway, a road tunnel and, of particular note, the Rove Canal Tunnel, were all built for one purpose: to provide the most rapid channels of communication between the harbour of Marseilles and Berre Lagoon. Regrettably, the Rove Tunnel, now partly collapsed, has not been used since 1963. The proximity of a great metropolis like Marseilles was bound to have an influence on the development of this virtually deserted region. Stretching from L'Estaque to Cape Couronne, the Côte Bleue, or Blue Coast, with deep inlets and white cliffs crowned with tousled pins and shimmering oak, became a popular leisure spot. **L'Estaque** was one of the haunts of the great artists of the end of the last century. The poet Saint-Pol-Roux and the writer Zola were often seen here, along with Cézanne, Dufy and Braque, who all came to capture the unique luminosity of its skies. Now an industrial suburb of Marseilles, the little town has, inevitably, lost some of its former charm. While the narrow inlets of **Niolon** and **La Vesse** plunge into the depths of their turquoise blue waters, the little fishing port of **Carry-le-Rouet** has become a lovely seaside resort, like **Sausset-les-Pins** and **Carro**, hidden among the rustling foliage of sweetly scented pinewoods.

Niolon Inlet

Berre Lagoon

Shaped rather like a butterfly's wing, the open expanses of Berre Lagoon are home to quarrelsome birds and light breezes. Its shallow waters cover a large natural depression, whose soft curves are echoed in the rounded forms of the surrounding limestone hills. Lending itself quite naturally to a gentle life of peace and quiet, the lagoon has, from the very earliest of times, been a much favoured dwelling place, and, as if to prove it, the site still boasts the remains of rocky Neolithic and protohistoric shelters, and Gallic *oppida*.

Situated on the edge of the vast urban expanses of Marseilles, Berre Lagoon was soon invaded by the city's spreading industrial suburbs, and, as port and oil-refining facilities sprang up along its banks, its delicate ecological balance began to be threatened. Fortunately, the foresight and courage of certain environmental groups have made it possible to reverse this alarming trend, and today, examined and analysed regularly, the lagoon has once more become a privileged site of outstanding natural beauty.

In spite of its complex network of canals, **Martigues** is still, at heart, a quiet little town. The waters of the lagoon, calmed and smoothed into luminous glassiness, capture the bright colours of boats and shutters in long undulating images in the *Miroir aux Oiseaux*, the Birds' Looking Glass. Dating from the 17th century, the Church of the Madeleine, dedicated to Mary Magdalene, has a well-preserved baroque facade. Across the water, in the Ferrières district, the Ziem Museum houses the works of this local painter who, having lived and worked in Martigues, bequeathed more than thirty of his paintings to the town. In 1972, a suspension bridge was built across the Caronte Canal to bear the motorway and its incessant stream of traffic.

Saint-Mitre-les-Remparts bears the most striking feature of its site in its name. The long

Martigues: The Ziem Museum - *Martigues Mosque* by Ziem

fortified wall of ramparts that surrounds the village is pierced by two fine, well-preserved gates. On a steep-sided knoll, overlooking the blue-grey expanses of the lagoons that surround it, the ruins of the oppidum on the **archeological site of Saint-Blaise** reveal some of the secrets of the long history of the peoples who, well before the arrival of the Romans, occupied and defended these strategic heights. Built in the 12th century, the tiny Saint Blaise's Chapel stands next to the ruins of an even older church. At **Istres**, the Arles Gate leads to the old town centre along narrow, sloping streets lined with 17th and 18th century houses. Built originally to watch and guard, the perched village of **Miramas-le-Vieux** still hides behind ramparts and fortified gates, and still enjoys a fine view, between the light branches of olive trees and the heavy boughs of fig trees, down to the glittering blue waters of Berre Lagoon.

The exterior of **Saint-Chamas'** baroque church is quite unique. Designed around a central *pietà*, which is usually found only as part of a church's interior decor, the facade is lent an altogether original look by its solid wood sculptured tympanum. The curved forms characteristic of the baroque style are to be found in the church's every detail, even in the architecture of its bell tower. Worn into horizontal seams and hollowed out into cave-dwellings, the cliff that runs along by the banks of the lagoon rises above the quiet port and its dancing boats. Just outside Saint-Chamas, **Flavien Bridge** stands solidly astride the Touloubre, a fine pair of triumphal arches marking either side of its single span. Ancient tracks left long ago by passing chariots can still be seen in the great white stones that pave its deck. The elaborately decorated arches take up the favorite themes of Augustus' imperial monarchy: foliated patterns, eagles, and gentle lions, leaning on their front paws, rumps raised in a long feline stretch. And an inscription recalls what would seem to be the fairly obvious fact that it was Flavius who built this – Flavien – Bridge.

Saint Blaise's Chapel

I N D E X